Near a Plantation

NEAR A PLANTATION
Free Villages of Barbados
1840–1945

Woodville Marshall

The University of the West Indies Press
Mona • St Augustine • Cave Hill • Global • Five Islands

First published in Jamaica, 2024 by
The University of the West Indies Press
7A Gibraltar Hall Road,
The UWI, Mona Campus,
Kingston 7, Jamaica
www.uwipress.com

© 2024, Woodville Marshall
ISBN: 978-976-640-961-6 (paperback)
       978-976-640-962-3 (epub)

A catalogue record of this book is available from
the National Library of Jamaica.

The University of the West Indies Press has no responsibility for the persistence or accuracy of URLs for external or third-party internet websites referred to in this publication and does not guarantee that any content on such websites is, or will remain, accurate or appropriate.

Cover and Book Design by Christina Moore Fuller
Cover image courtesy of the Barbados Museum and Historical Society

Printed and Bound in the United States of America

Contents

List of Tables vii

List of Maps ix

Acknowledgements xi

1: The Project, Its Sources and Method of Analysis 1

2: The Context of Early Free Village Development 13

3: The First Free Villages 26

4: Free Village Expansion 48

5: Remittances and Plantation Subdivision 67

6: Role of Free Village and Villagers 86

Notes 103

Appendix: Free Villages, Number, Approximate Size and
   Date of Formation 109

Bibliography 127

Index 135

List of Tables

Table 2.1: The Pre-Emancipation Villages 19

Table 3.1: Location, Estimated Number, Type and Size of the First Free Villages 28

Table 3.2: Holdings at The Nursery by 1875 33

Table 3.3: Table of Estimated Number and Size of Bequest Villages 36

Table 3.4: Estimates of the Number and Size of Speculators' Villages 43

Table 4.1: New Free Villages, Approximate Numbers, 1870–1905 48

Table 4.2: Distribution of Villages According to Number of Holdings 51

Table 5.1: Villages: Number and Estimates of Acreage and Number of Holdings, 1905–45 67

Table 5.2: Holdings in Third Phase Villages 78

Table 6.1: Tally of Villages 86

List of Maps

Map 2.1: Physiographic Areas of Barbados 16

Map 3.1: The First Free Villages 27

Map 4.1: The Increase in Number of Free Villages 49

Map 5.1: Free Villages by 1945 68

Acknowledgements

This modest attempt to reconstruct the formation of Barbadian free villages has been made possible as a result of various types of encouragement and assistance. First, I wish to thank the staff of the Barbados Department of Archives who, over many years, provided me with full access to the mass of materials that was in their safekeeping. Second, I wish to acknowledge the co-operation that was offered by the editors of the *Journal of Caribbean History* and of the *Journal of the Barbados Museum & Historical Society*, who published earlier versions of sections of the manuscript. Third, and most important of all, I wish to acknowledge the impetus that has been provided by two of our eminent scholars on the Caribbean. After all, it was almost sixty years ago that both Raymond Smith and Sidney Mintz suggested that scholars of the Caribbean, especially historians, should be "teasing out" the details of the establishment of free villages because such reconstructions could "prove valuable in understanding the social organization of the contemporary communities themselves".

ONE
The Project, Its Sources and Method of Analysis

This book is the by-product of what should have been a study of the development of smallholdings (or the peasantry) in the British Caribbean.[1] That larger project was abandoned partly because of how difficult it was to access some of the probable sources and mainly because researchers uncovered two early free villages, Rock Hall and Bridgefield, at an early phase during the research in Barbados. That finding, briefly described in a conference paper, in a film, in a public lecture and in a journal article,[2] seemed important for at least two reasons. First, if the formation of those villages represented more than isolated cases, then there was a clear suggestion that many more of the formerly enslaved population may have established communities which were not tied to the sugar plantations; and second, that the development would point not only to the existence of smallholding but could also demonstrate that, in some respects, post-slavery social developments in Barbados were not different from those found in territories where resources of land were not limited. In short, it seemed that the conventional wisdom, loudly echoed by post-slavery historians, that no free villages were created in Barbados[3] needed serious questioning.

That tentative conclusion gained traction because of what a review of the literature on free villages seemed to reveal. First, few historians and social anthropologists, with the notable exceptions of Michel-Rolph Trouillot, Jean Besson and possibly Catherine Hall, seemed to have followed the advice that had been tendered in the 1950s by two of the pioneers in free village studies. Both Raymond Smith and Sidney Mintz, social anthropologists, had suggested that historians and problem-oriented social scientists should engage both in the "teasing out" of the histories of these social organizations and in the painting of the "exceedingly complex" picture of free villages. In those ways, they said, scholars would help to ensure that an understanding of the social organization of the contemporary communities would become clearer and also that there would be comprehension of the connections of free villages with the wider social, economic and political context.[4]

Second, the scholarly work on post-slavery, though "vast", seemed somewhat general in its coverage of rural life. It identified the drive to form free villages, the number, the locations and the types of those villages. Therefore, the work of William Green, Gisela Eisner and Thomas Holt; of Alan Adamson, Walter Rodney, and Brian Moore; of Raphael Sebastien and Susan Craig did significantly add to that volume of information that had been earlier produced by Hugh Paget and Douglas Hall, Rawle Farley and Allan Young. But most of the later studies (like the earlier ones) were territory-based and therefore did not address similarities and differences between the developments in different localities. Even more important, most of those studies cannot be regarded as the teasing of those details which are necessary to reconstruct the history of those communities and their relationship with other social sectors. For example, the studies provided little detailed information about who bought and who sold land, about the many processes of negotiation and the choice of particular locations, about age profiles, kinship networks, religious and political activities, about active association with specific localities, about the content of villagers' lives and about the extent to which villages displayed elements of socio-cultural autonomy and functioned as separate communities.[5]

Third, the historians, seemingly tied to formulations about relative population density and its impact on plantation labour supplies, paid little attention to the details of what transpired in Barbados after apprenticeship was curtailed in 1838. William Green in 1976 asserted that no free villages existed; Claude Levy in 1980 never mentioned their existence; and even Henderson Carter in 2012 only made fleeting references to their formation. Therefore, it seemed a truism that if it could be shown that Barbadian free villages existed in large numbers, then it followed that those villages and villagers may have played active roles in whatever social transformations occurred during their existence.

This small study has two objectives. First, it tries to reveal that a variant of free villages did flourish in Barbados, particularly after 1870.

Second, in establishing some of the details of free village existence, it makes possible a painting of rural life in Barbados and the subregion.

Sources

This study of the Barbadian variant of free villages has been necessarily determined by the quality and quantity of available sources. Those sources, official or otherwise, can hardly be considered as comprehensive. Free village development received limited attention at the highest level mainly because elite groups believed smallhold landholding, especially in the hands of the formerly enslaved, was harmful to agriculture in general and to a plantation-based economy in particular. Therefore, it was only when villagers' activity seemed to pose a threat to public health, to public order and to vital ongoing economic activity that top officials and planters warned of free villagers' presence, especially of the danger of creating a second Haiti. It follows, then, that before the 1940s, the main sources on free villages are found in non-specific records, in basic civil registration data (registers of baptism, marriages and burials), in wills and deeds and in the data on voting and tax payment, in particular in the records pertaining to those who paid land taxes that were collected at the parochial level.

Official and Semi-official Sources

The various sources fall into the following categories:

Official Records

Officials at the Colonial Office, because of their general oversight of colonies, did require, early in the piece, that the governors (obviously through the main civil servants) provide information about the likely impact of village development on the plantations' labour force. Therefore, stipendiary magistrates, in all colonies where formerly enslaved labourers constituted the labour force, were required to provide information in their semi-annual reports on tenancy arrangements on the plantations, on the extent of the success that had accompanied the efforts of the formerly enslaved to establish themselves as freeholders, on "the rising up of new hamlets and villages", and on the "supposed" effect of those developments on the labour market and on the production of export staples.⁶

This was potentially a solid source because it could have provided hard evidence that free villages existed before 1853, the date when the British government ended its financial support of stipendiary magistrates. But those sources are somewhat disappointing. Scraps of information on smallhold land development and village formation were reported from the parishes of St Michael, Christ Church and St John, no doubt because the magistrates, apparently satisfied that emancipation had registered little or no impact on the supply of labour for the sugar plantations, relied heavily on information that was furnished by their social *confreres*, the planters. Therefore, apart from what was occasionally reported on the formation of the villages of Rock Hall and Bridgefield in the parish of St Thomas, those reports suggest that no hamlets or villages were arising. Consequently, the police magistrates assigned to the parish of Christ Church regrettably did not not fully report on the action and effects of William Reece's bequest at the plantations of Gibbons and Pilgrim Place.

List of Landowners of One Acre and Upwards

However, it is possible that the Colonial Office's monitoring of the labour situation may have produced one useful piece of information. In May/June 1847, the governor was requested to provide a list of all persons who owned one acre and upwards. This list is useful because it provides information on the spread of landownership (which may have occurred before August 1838) in all but one of the eleven parishes during the first ten years of full slave emancipation. (No response seems to have arrived from the parish of St Andrew.) But here again, the police magistrates could have done a better job. While they may have identified all of the landowners in the stated category, they did not, except in the case of the parish of St Michael, supply the addresses of all the landowners, and in many instances, the addresses of small landowners are omitted. But there is a larger problem with the list. Identification of the village areas is further obstructed by the governor's request for the names of owners of one acre and upwards. The problem is that even if the addresses of all landowners were all supplied, we might not be able to fully plot the early incidence of village development because, as will be shown, most of the small landowners owned less than one acre.⁷

"Principal" Villages, 1885

This listing of "principal" villages was provoked by the work of the Water Supply Commission. That commission, appointed by the governor in July 1885, had been charged with ascertaining "the best way of providing a supply of pure water for all parts of the island". In order to do its work, the commission requested each vestry (the equivalent of local government) to identify, among other matters, "the principal villages", as well as the approximate population of these villages. In response, the chairmen of the vestries of nine parishes identified some ninety-two villages but, as to be expected, only four parishes provided estimates of the villages' population.

But there is a more serious problem with the data. It is not clear whether the chairmen of the vestries fully understood that they were to name only the principal villages; there was no clear definition of what "principal" meant; and there was no way of telling whether the comment from the St George Vestry chairman could be generalized. He reported that "as far as can be estimated", the twenty-one villages in his parish "contain about two-thirds of the whole population of the parish". However, it must be noted that preparation of the lists did indicate that the existence of village development, though not publicly acknowledged, was established in the consciousness of those who mattered.[8]

Surveys of Peasant Agriculture

Those surveys of peasant agriculture came late, not until 1929/30. These were spearheaded by the Colonial Office and the Colonial Development and Welfare Commission in order to provide information for the Sugar Commission of 1929 and for the Moyne Commission of 1939, which were examining the effects of prolonged depression on the sugar industry. It might be said that the surveys marked the beginnings of an ideological shift: these surveys were the first time that peasants/villagers were being discussed, not as a possible nuisance or a burden, but as possibly effective members of the society.

The first survey, *The Condition of Peasant Agriculture in Barbados*, was conducted by C.C. Skeete in 1930, and it was the first time that peasant agriculture (and villages) were receiving positive official attention.

The study is useful, particularly for what it reveals about the means of acquiring land, about the extent to which a small farming community was in existence, and especially about what Skeete termed "the predominating system" in peasant farming. But the survey is deficient in determining how the peasants came into existence and about the full extent of village development. For example, it is somewhat surprising that Skeete, after an island-wide tour, could conclude that "the more important holdings" only numbered seventy-seven.[9]

The second survey, *Peasant Agriculture in Barbados*, undertaken by M. Halcrow and J.M. Cave in 1944/1947, was something of a contrast. The authors, as Skeete had done, naturally paid attention to peasant crops, to manuring, irrigation, etc., but, unlike Skeete, their "facts and figures" were far more complete and organized. They did imply a definition of a village, they did try to count all the villages in the island, and they obviously utilized the parish rate books as sources for the location, size and number of those villages. The survey is therefore an important source, but one might want to quibble about three matters.

First is the dating of village development. Basically, they claimed that free village development started in the late nineteenth century. But subsequent research has established there was no basis for the statement that "there was practically no development of Africans as peasant farmers until about the year 1895". Second is the implied definition of a village. The authors seemed to have taken the view that ownership of a lot meant occupancy of that lot. However, a question arises when an individual owns multiple lots in different locations and resides on none of them. In such cases, the individual might be counted more than once. The third quibble concerns the number of villages. The authors do say that the number of villages was 616 (inclusive of sixty-eight, with each containing less than five holdings), but they do not supply a clear basis for excluding from the appendix the names of the two-hundred-plus villages that each contained five lots.[10]

Civil Registration Records

The vital registration records are of limited importance. These may facilitate the tracking of individuals, particularly in cases of bequests. Moreover, this becomes important if a formerly enslaved person, with only one name, became baptized or married and in the process acquired a second name. Similarly, the censuses, taken at ten-year intervals after 1851, are not as helpful as these might have been. For example, the census takers in 1851 indicate that the "only" villages that existed were the four villages in the parish of St Thomas. Unfortunately, they either ignored or seemed to be unaware of similar developments taking place in the parishes of St Michael, Christ Church and St John. However, in 1911 and 1921, they did notice that "extensive villages" had been established outside of Bridgetown.

Taxpayers and Voters

Far more important were records of taxpayers and of those who did qualify to vote in a particular constituency. For example, because there was a property qualification for the exercise of the franchise, those records can help to identify those Rock Hall villagers who created the mini-political crisis in 1848/49. That episode does reveal the political potential of the new villagers. Equally important are the lists of those who paid the militia tax and the annual land tax. Because the militia tax was levied on those who owned at least an acre of land and because their addresses were also listed, it is possible therefore to establish the sites of some villages.[11]

However, there were at least three reasons why the list of those who paid land tax have to be put in a special category. Every owner of a lot, which could be as small as one-sixteenth of an acre, was liable for taxation; this tax was levied and collected by officials at the individual parish level; and, of course, the location of the lot had to be specified. It follows then, that, provided the lots were formally registered, those records are the most reliable means of tracking the location, the number and the size of villages. The problem was, however, that those records, in most instances, have not survived in any great number, especially for the late nineteenth century.[12]

Wills and Deeds

These documents, in the absence of a complete set of land tax records, are the best means of reconstructing the development of free villages, and these are stored in the Barbados Department of Archives. The wills are vital for determining which villages might be denominated as bequest and family villages because the donors, the legatees and the quantity of land are specified. The problem is, however, that in a society where the making of wills may not have been a working-class pre-occupation, there can be no certainty about how much land was being held on customary tenure. The same point can be made with more cogency with respect to deeds. While it may be possible to track landownership through registration of ownership of a particular lot, difficulties must arise when the legal owner is unknown and particularly when the ownership is unregistered. But, it must be emphasized, that in the absence of credible oral accounts, then the written record, incomplete as it might be, must be the most reliable source.[13]

Other Source Materials

A few newspapers, some surveyors' plats and some scholarly studies have addressed aspects of free village development. Attention to these can be brief because, in general, village development was ignored by newspaper editors and other commentators when it was not seen as the cause of societal backwardness.

Newspapers

The *Liberal* was the one newspaper that provided any extended commentary on a village. This was not surprising because that newspaper was owned and edited by Samuel Jackman Prescod who also founded the Liberal Party, which actively campaigned among the villagers. Therefore, the newspaper's commentary and report on the fierce election campaign in the parish of St Thomas in 1848/49 *and* on the controverted election which resulted do provide at least a glimpse of the political potential that resided in villages.[14] In addition, it might be worth noticing that, in February 1911, the *Barbados Advocate* chided its rival, the *Agricultural Reporter*, for its opposition to small landholding development, and asserted that "the occasional cutting up of an estate affords a safety valve to the thrifty peasantry".[15]

Surveyors' Plats

The surviving plats are potentially useful sources on the size and location of some villages and on the identities of the original occupants of the villages. The point must be stated cautiously because the archive, being in private hands, cannot be fully assessed. That archive is (or was) apparently in the keeping of a senior land surveyor who then passed on the collection of plats to the senior land surveyor in the succeeding generation. Limited acquaintance with the archive would suggest that it would be particularly useful where land surveys were commissioned in preparation for the subdivision of a plantation or of a substantial portion of a plantation but not where the separation of small acreages, the dominant species of small landownership, did or does occur.[16] But the important point is that it is not clear whether that archive is still being maintained or whether it is still in Barbados.

Scholarly Work

The little scholarly work that has been so far done on Barbadian free villages has been produced, not by historians, but mainly by social anthropologists. Therefore, some attention has to be paid to the work of Constance Sutton, Sidney Greenfield, Christine Barrow, and George and Sharon Gmelch, most of whom have tested the validity of particular theories in a single village. Most of this work is useful, particularly to the extent that it presents a reliable guide to the formation of individual villages, but it might be suggested that in all cases the historical frame for the work could be improved.

Finally, attention might be drawn to the research that has been conducted by a few undergraduate students at the Barbados campus of the University of the West Indies. This source is mentioned last, not because it contains unimportant information, but because the circumstances of its preparation may render it difficult to access. In any case, the research that was conducted by Ann Franklin and Etheline Taitt on the subdivision of two plantations (Mount Clapham and Chimborazo) did establish the importance of remittances in the later stages of free village development.[17]

Method of Analysis

The method of analysis, as should be already apparent, was largely determined by the uneven quality and limited quantity of the available sources. Because record-keeping in Barbados, or rather the maintenance of the record, was somewhat of a haphazard affair before the 1960s, there was no series, as in places like Jamaica, which provided comprehensive information on the acquisition of small landholdings for the period that was being examined. Therefore, limits to the analysis were imposed because the parish rate books have disappeared for many parishes. Even when these rate books were recovered, problems arose because the location of the taxed land was sometimes not recorded. Some attempt has therefore been made to fill in those gaps by close scrutiny of wills and deeds, but it should be obvious that in communities where attention to legal formalities was probably the exception rather than the rule because of a perception of costs and because of limited educational opportunities, then there could be no guarantee that such scrutiny has sufficiently ensured the filling of all the large gaps in the written record.

Defining the Free Village

This issue presented few problems because it seemed appropriate to adopt the implied definition that had been put into currency in November 1838 by William Knibb.[18] Basically, what this Baptist missionary in Jamaica called a free village was a cluster of houses placed on land that was controlled by the occupants of the houses, the formerly enslaved, where their occupancy (of house and land) was not conditional on the rendering of labour services to any planter. Obviously, as some anthropologists have indicated, such a bare definition does not accord with traditional usage; and the Barbadian (and Caribbean) village seems to differ from the "village" that can be found on the ground in Europe, Asia and in parts of Latin America because its formation is somewhat haphazard and its settlement pattern does not include a recognizable centre or plaza.[19] But the point is that these Barbadian settlements encouraged social intermingling, whether at church, rum shop or stand pipe; that the residents described these settlements as villages or districts; and that observers, whether they were foreign-derived or local, did classify those clusters as villages. Therefore, there is abundant reason to classify the clusters as the local variant of free villages.

The related point is how large the cluster of houses must be in order for the designation of village to be applied. Given the fact that Barbadian households contain at least five persons per house, it seems reasonable to accept Halcrow and Cave's working definition that the minimum number of houses in the cluster, except in rare cases, should be five.[20] Therefore, it is those clusters of houses and holdings in specific geographical areas that are identified as villages in the course of this study. It must be noticed, however, that scattered clusters of houses in one geographical area do often qualify as a single village.

Periods/Phases in Free Village Development

Close scrutiny of free village development over a century indicated that the development was deeply influenced at different times by certain socio-economic factors. To begin with (and continuing) was the evident desire of the newly freed to actualize their emancipation by establishing or regaining a measure of control over their labour power; and this meant escaping from the plantation tenantries and establishing settlements on their own land. Secondly, those efforts were aided by the planters' misfortunes which became pronounced when free trade and bounty-fed beet sugar virtually destroyed the market for cane sugar; and this meant some easing of the planters' tight grip on the island's limited land resources. Thirdly, remittances from migrants, particularly those who went to Panama to assist in building the Panama Canal, prompted plantation subdivision; and this meant both a limited re-distribution of what had been plantation land and a significant alteration of settlement patterns.

Therefore, it seemed sensible to organize the materials so that these factors and consequences of these factors could be made explicit. It followed then that the main story, after some introductory remarks, could be told in three chapters. These would be free village development before the full impact of free trade and beet sugar was experienced; the clear effects of the planters' misfortunes on additional appropriation of land by small landowners; and the influence of remittances in promoting plantation subdivision. The study would then conclude with a discussion of the role of villagers and villages.

Fitting the Pieces Together

What was involved was a close search of the available sources for any quantitative data, in particular, on the formation of free villages. This was intensive, especially for the first phase, because except for the parish of St Michael in 1852, the parish rate books did not seem to exist. Therefore, deeds and wills had to consulted, but it is almost certain that these did not provide a full picture of land alienation or purchase. It is very likely that there has been an under-reporting of the number of villages that appeared during this initial phase. The situation was cleaner for the succeeding phases. Some parish rate books are available for five parishes, and this made it easier to plot village formation in those parishes; but it also has meant that rough estimates had to be made about the number of holdings and of the size of the villages for which no rate books apparently existed. This was particularly true for the second phase, but it was not the case for the third phase. The reason for this was that Halcrow and Cave, who obviously had access to all the parish rate books, could report in 1947 on what their team had collected for the years, 1945–46.

This study can therefore be regarded as a compendium. It lists all the free villages that were formed, providing information on where the villages were formed and on the approximate size (number of holdings and acreage) of those villages. It addresses the constraints on the formation of the villages, and it explains the factors that assisted the formation of free villages. Finally, it attempts to assess the role of the villages and villagers.

TWO
The Context of Early Free Village Development

The Barbadian variants of free villages were legal entities almost to the extent that these were social realities. Those clusters of houses may not have completely shielded residents from what Knibb had called the "treachery, scorn and treachery" of the planters, but the creation of those clusters relieved the residents of a critical legal compulsion. The clusters, sometimes called "districts", represented the domiciles of those formerly enslaved individuals that were located, not on plantation land, but on land that was *fully* controlled by former residents of plantation tenantries. Those clusters of largely wooden houses, with each cluster containing at least five houses, were, as David Lowenthal later observed, usually located along the highways, "occasionally two or three deep but usually strung out singly on both sides of the white coral roads". Those clusters, he found, generally "focus around crossroads where a few shops, a street lamp, and maybe a chapel are to be found, are extraordinarily compact; houses touch, or almost touch, and may have only a few square yards for a yard or a garden".[1] Such clustering did naturally provide continuing opportunities for social interaction, for sharing, for the joint involvement in the rituals that were associated with birth, living and dying – in short, with the moulding of community spirit.

But what principally distinguished those clusters from the old "nigger yards" and the new plantation tenantries was the fact that occupants of the houses and lands were under no legal requirement to provide labour services on any specific plantation because they were the legal owners of the new property. It is true that the existing economic circumstances – the limited employment options imposed by both plantation domination of the economy and by the inability of most villagers to convert themselves into full-time small farmers – meant that plantation labour remained the chief means of subsistence for all the emancipated, villagers or not; but free village development gave the villagers a degree of control over where and the extent to which their labour would be employed. In other words, villagers had a measure of control over their labour power because they could become *strangers* on any plantation that chose to employ them; and they could thus earn a higher wage than the *residents* of plantation tenantries, who were forced to pay rent in one form or other. Therefore, even though the Barbadian free village, like free villages in several Caribbean countries, could be seen as forming a symbiotic economic relationship with the plantation,[2] it must also be emphasized that these villagers now had some control over the disposal of their labour power, which might be another way of saying that village development could be represented as emancipation in action.

The other relevant point is the identification of the existence of free villages. This becomes a problem for a number of reasons. Villages are hardly mentioned in official correspondence; the villages merit only passing reference in the regular censuses; housing surveys were not commissioned before the 1940s; comprehensive listing of the number of villages was not attempted until 1946/47; and not surprisingly, those settlements did not generally feature on maps until the 1950s. This means that recovery of information on free village development has to be based, partly on oral tradition, but mainly on a perusal of deeds, wills and lists of taxpayers. But this also raises a minor problem. Since the existence of villages has to be abstracted from records of ownership and occupancy of holdings in particular locations, one has to assume that possession equated to occupancy; and therefore, a problem arises if an individual possessed more than one holding in different locations, and might not even have resided on any of the holdings that he or she might own. This, however, might be a minor matter; the point remains that identification of clusters of houses and land holdings that are located *outside* of the plantation was the clearest indication of the presence of free villages.

What seems so obvious that it needs not to be over-emphasized was the emancipated people's interest in the acquisition of some land. Tilling of the soil was the main skill that they possessed, and they had turned that skill to advantage in the cultivation of the small gardens that surrounded houses in the *nigger yard*, and as a result they had carved out for themselves a niche in the internal market in ground provisions and fruit which the authorities had tried in vain to curtail.[3] Moreover, with the limited employment opportunities outside of plantation labour that were inevitably available, they were anxious to exploit their limited skills in their own interest and to exercise their newly gained freedom by investigating whatever landowning could provide. Therefore, there should be no surprise that John Davy, who lived in the island between 1845 and 1848, should write: "for the coloured race have a great desire to possess land, are ready to pay high prices for small portions, have a peculiar facility in locating themselves on their purchases, and are not impeded by expensive legal processes".[4]

Free villages were established, as will be shown, but it was obvious that this development was hampered by constraints that were both environmental and human. Indeed, on the face of it, there seemed to be little or no land space available to accommodate what planters feared in these formerly slave societies, that is, a massive exodus from the sugar plantations. First, it must be noticed that Barbados was a small, densely populated island. It contained only 106, 470 acres in what was for the most part open terrain. More important, the portions of that acreage that were considered to be arable had been appropriated and cleared of forest cover by the 1660s, and with the possible exception of Turner's Hall Wood, the only small patches of "woods" that remained were those that were preserved for apparently ornamental purposes on several plantations. Therefore, Barbados, unlike its neighbours in the Windward Islands, unlike Jamaica, and especially unlike Trinidad and British Guiana in the British Caribbean, possessed little or no Crown Land, no waste land, no abandoned plantations, hardly any mountains, creeks or rivers that could sustain human existence. The only small portions of land that remained sparsely settled were to be found in the land deemed marginal to the sugar-cane enterprise; and this land could be found on the coastal plains, mainly in the Scotland District and Below the Cliff (in the north-eastern and northern parishes of St John, St Joseph, St Andrew, and St Lucy) and at Foul Bay, Penny Hole, and Below the Rock (in the southern parishes of St Philip and Christ Church).[5]

Clearly, the main sugar cane planters, driven by the promise and impact of the so-called Sugar Revolution, had remained resolved to maximize their enjoyment of the sweets that the sugar industry could bring.

Map 2.1: Physiographic Areas of Barbados

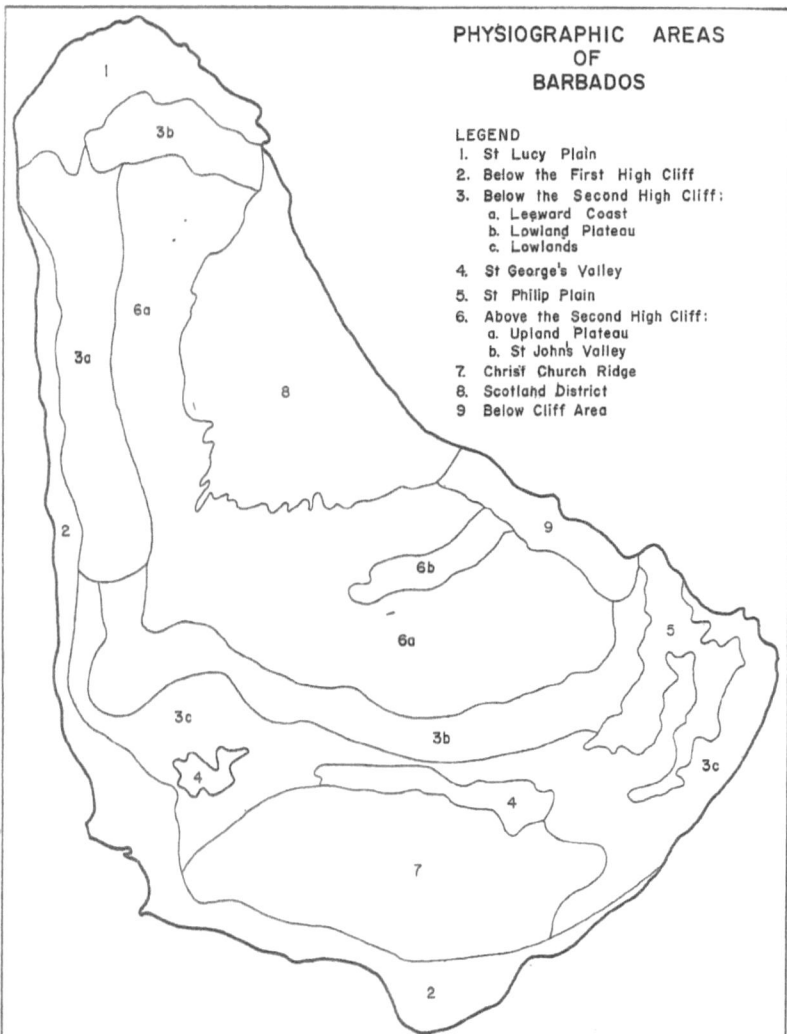

Source: Vernon and Carrol, *Soil and Land-Use Surveys No. 18 Barbados*

Second, the island was one of the most densely populated countries on earth. In 1829, the total population, according to Robert Schomburgk, was 103,007, and in 1845 that population was estimated by Governor Sir Charles Grey as not less than 130,000 and fast increasing.[6] But two significant points might be noticed about those statistics. First, the population density of one person to less than one acre did exceed that of China and was only exceeded by Malta in all European countries. Secondly, and equally important, was the composition of the population. At least 80 per cent were Africa-derived or Africa-descended, those individuals who until 1834 had been enslaved mainly on the sugar plantations and who were perceived by planters and their apologists as the perennial labourers on the plantations.

The third significant factor naturally followed: all the arable land had been appropriated. That acreage, amounting to about ninety-five thousand to one hundred thousand acres, was locked up in the 508 plantations and in the 1,367 smaller landed units that were known as *places*. This mainly plantation development had become the prime form of land appropriation which had been triggered by the so-called Sugar Revolution of the 1640s. That successful search for a remunerative export staple had installed a sugar-cane economy which created the base for the almost complete political power that its owners did wield. Indeed, as already indicated, there was some *rab* land which accommodated a few "poor white" settlements/villages, for example, at Church Village and Foul Bay in the parish of St Philip, at Below Rock and Sargeants Village in the parish of Christ Church, at Sweet Bottom/Sweet Vale in the parish of St George, and at Triopath in the parish of St Andrew (see table 2.1). These were some of the sites of the earliest villages, the settlements which owed their existence, ever since the late seventeenth century, to two developments. The first of those developments was the presence of time-expired indentured servants and their descendants *and* of militia tenants, who had been largely exiled to these relatively infertile segments of the country.[7] The second explanation of the presence of a few of these villages, also identified in table 2.1, was that they were the effects of the bequests that had been occasionally made by white planters to their enslaved paramours and to the children born of those unions.[8]

However, in the context of free village development, special notice must be taken of the *places*. These were the small properties that had survived the agglomeration that had been triggered by the conversion to general cane sugar production; and *places* therefore represented important nodes in the settlement history of the island. These small properties were in a real sense the remnants of the original landowning pattern because the early English settlers did not generally establish large plantations during the first twenty years of colonization. As a result, smallhold landownership (which led to the coining of the term "ten-acre men") seemed to have been the norm until most of the holdings of these small landholders were integrated into larger units when the sugar cane industry became established during and after the 1640s. But the important point, as Richard Dunn has insisted,[9] was that these units did not completely disappear, mainly because inheritance practices, particularly those that featured bequests of landed property to daughters and to younger sons, made the presence of *places* a permanent feature of the landscape. But the more relevant point was that, in general, it seems that the *places*, rather than established plantations, became the principal sites of the new villages that were established during the later nineteenth century, that is, before remittances prompted the subdivision of some medium-sized and large plantations.

In such a situation, then, the human factor was likely to be a key constraint on village development. This was so because the planters owned the land that would form villages, and their general reluctance to part with any of it, except for tiny parcels, did frustrate many ambitions. The elite planters said loudly and often, particularly in the District Agricultural Societies, that small farms had would produce "evil effects". These farming practices, they said, were "at variance with all rational views of a prosperous country", and these small farms had a tendency both to withdraw labour from larger plantations and "to deteriorate agriculture". Therefore, they urged their fellows to adopt a policy of "concentration of capital and labour" as the best means of exploiting the island's agricultural resources.[10]

Table 2.1: The Pre-Emancipation Villages

Parish	Certain	Probable
St Philip	Foul Bay, Padmore Village**	Parish Land, Penny Hole, Merricks
	Six Roads, Church Village	Long Bay
Christ Church	Bath Village**, Below Rock,	
	Cotton Coast, Sargeants Village**	
St Andrew	Boscobel*, Chalky Mount	
St George	Sweet Bottom**, Market Hill	
St James	Hoyte's Village**, Payne's Bay	
St Joseph	Cleavers Hill, Crab Hole, Surinam	
St John	Martin's Bay (Below the Cliff)	
St Lucy	Pie Corner	
St Thomas	Irish Town	
St Michael		Indian River

*Also in St Peter   **Early Bequest Villages
Sources: Register of Baptisms, deeds and wills in the Barbados Department of Archives

This was, in essence, a declaration of self-interest and commitment to the social *status quo*. After all, those planters owned the land on which the sugar cane industry was based; that industry, because it was the mainstay of the economy of the island, gave them their lofty social and economic positions; the sugar cane industry was, for them, the *raison d'etre* for the Barbados colony; cane sugar could only maintain its profitability, they believed, if the labour input into the industry remained plentiful, cheap and dependent; and since they were accustomed to having at their disposal such a labour force, and since that input was even more essential in the face of competition from cheaper producers, it made perfect sense to them that Barbados should seek to retain what sustained their own positions and gave their portion of the cane sugar industry its competitive edge. Therefore, they were anxious to employ all means to keep the traditional labour force in Barbados and tied to the plantations.

Perhaps, one might notice that the colonial connection did provide an element of complication. On the one hand, it was becoming apparent, except to the purblind, that colonists' concerns did not heavily feature in metropolitan decision-making. Therefore, it seemed entirely probable that the British government, in seeking to maximize its own interests, might take action that would over time damage colonial prospects that were no longer of major interest to the metropolis. Examples of this tendency could be found in the abolition of the slave trade and of slavery despite colonial opposition, but of even greater significance was the growing embrace of free trade ideology, which was likely to benefit metropolitan consumers and merchants but would destroy a protected market and reduce if not eliminate profit margins for British Caribbean cane sugar producers.

On the other hand, it might be said, those dimming prospects for the Barbadian sugar cane industry, which might be termed the *misfortunes* of the planters, while these made the planters more strident in their opposition to village development and smallholding, did create some opportunities for those developments to take hold. It is therefore being suggested that reduced profit margins for local producers of cane sugar and the implied threat to an accustomed lifestyle might have tempted a few planters, especially smaller planters, to the seek short-term profit or relief in the alienation of a few acres of their plantation land. But, for all planters, large and small, there was immediately at hand the legislative means that could legally create their desirable objective.

The legislative action that was designed to preserve the presence of a plantation-dependent labour force was therefore what the Colonial Office called "a new form" to reproduce many of the evils associated with slavery.[11] This could be seen in much of that legislation on vagrancy, emigration, policing and labour contracts that was hastily drafted during apprenticeship and especially when that interlude was nearing an early end. Much of this draft legislation had to be modified on the insistence of the Colonial Office, but as Bentley Gibbs argues, the planter/legislators' actions were consistent with their opposition to the emancipation of enslaved people. They designed regulations or a system that "only men experienced in the techniques of slave control could invent and put into operation"; and it was equally obvious that the nature of the system was likely to be opposed by some, if not most, of the emancipated.[12]

Two issues were particularly relevant. The first was the planters' anti-emigration stance. Because of the high population density of Barbados, the planters in low-density colonies like Guyana (British Guiana) and Trinidad looked to Barbados, the high-density colony *par excellence*, for augmentation of their labour force. At the same time, the news that agricultural labourers in those colonies could earn wages that were at least double those that prevailed in Barbados was a standing temptation for emancipated Barbadians to emigrate. Therefore, the planters, through the legislature, used the specious claims that they were safeguarding the welfare of impotent families and helpless infants, as well as the health and safety of migrants, to limit emigration. They did this over time by mandating tickets-of-leave, by imposing fines on anyone who attempted to decoy or entice away children under sixteen years of age, by requiring emigration agents to obtain certificates to permit them to operate, and by imposing strict regulations particularly with regard to the transport and feeding of would-be emigrants.[13] The obvious point was not so much to prevent the accumulation of remittances which could (and did) enable family members of migrants to buy small lots of land, the bases of villages, as it was as to ensure that the planters did retain a dependent labour force. This was somewhat successful, as G.W. Roberts notes that no more than four thousand emigrants departed for Guyana and Trinidad between 1838 and 1842.[14]

Even more relevant was the implantation of the plantation tenantries or the located labourer system. The relevance arose because it could be argued that this was the immediate trigger for free village development. Those arrangements, which were drafted by the legislature, created an imposing block to smallholding which was the obvious prerequisite for village creation. Under this legislation, the newly freed, who were generally in need of shelter and wages, were permitted occupancy of house and a small piece of land on the plantations where they were attached, provided that all residents of any individual house remained under a legal obligation to perform labour services on the plantations to which they were attached, whenever those services were required. Moreover, they were paid wages which were usually reduced to cover the cost of the rent of house and ground, or they were charged a money-rent; they were liable to fines or imprisonment for non-appearance or other breaches of the contract; and they were liable to eviction at short notice if they were found guilty of infractions of the arrangements.[15] The point here was that the emancipated people could access what they needed most – shelter and wages – provided they sacrificed what was for them a major element of their emancipation, which was control over their own labour time. Therefore, there can be little wonder that Samuel Jackman Prescod told the *Anti-Slavery Reporter* that those arrangements constituted "a sort of civil bondage on the estates", and that W.G. Sewell, observing rural dynamics in 1859, declared that this system of tenancy-at-will made the labourer "virtually a slave".[16]

Therefore, too, there is every reason to conclude that those *contractual* arrangements sparked the industrial conflict on many plantations in 1838–40 that Henderson Carter has clearly described.[17] Indeed, the nature of those conflicts may have strengthened a desire to decamp plantation residence wherever possible, but it might be a little simplistic to suggest that free village development over the century may have been mainly sparked by those terms of engagement. After all, the emancipated people in whatever territory they lived, all of them possessing the similar experience of enslavement, particularly the possibilities that could be glimpsed in the provision ground/marketing complex, always displayed a determination to make emancipation more complete. It could be suggested, then, that they were not so much resisting the pressure to perform agricultural labour as protesting against the terms on which that labour would be compensated.

The creation of this system of recruitment could no doubt be justified (as it was) as an arrangement that guaranteed to the planters a reliable and sufficient labour supply. But the question, at least from a modern-day perspective, must arise: with a dense population, with virtually all the land already appropriated, with emigration outlets that were increasingly blocked, how could most of the emancipated, with their limited skills and probable attachment to the sites where their families had lived and died, earn a living except by labouring on the plantations on terms that the existing economic circumstances dictated? But no doubt, however, custom and political weight – not economic rationality – carried the day; and this was apparently to the benefit of those planters, perhaps the majority, who by their earlier treatment of the enslaved population, could expect a payback. But the obvious point was this: the planters were declaring opposition to small landholdings, and in this matter, they held the upper hand for a long time.

Moreover, there was limited inducement for the emancipated to settle in the few existing village sites. Those sites, identified in table 2.1, numbered no more than twenty-five, and they were generally located, as already indicated, on the margins of the plantations, on the sea-coast plains and on shallow, rocky soil, on land that was perceived as not capable of intensive cultivation. Therefore, those sites, small as they were, could not have accommodated an influx, even if many of the emancipated wished to decamp there. What also might have made the sites less attractive to the emancipated was the complexion and racial history of most of the inhabitants of those enclaves. Most of those villagers were white because they were the descendants of indentured servants and militia tenants, and this feature, in a colour-conscious society, assumed some significance. Even though the low social status of those villagers may have led to some miscegenation, there may still have been the fact or at least the perception of colour prejudice.

However, these constraints on free village development were put into full perspective by the results of a survey of the price of whatever small portions of land that did become available. Scrutiny of deeds that recorded the price of small lots at ten locations during the 1840s and 1850s revealed that the price was on average about £80 per acre, ranging from a low of about £55 per acre at Good Intent in the parish of St George to a high of £125 per acre at Cherry Grove in the parish of St John; but there were instances when the price reached £400 to £700 per acre.[18] What makes those prices striking, first of all, is the comparison with what obtained in some other Caribbean territories. For example, in Guyana, Trinidad, and the Windward Islands, uncultivated land was virtually free of cost, and in Jamaica, land prices ranged between £2 per acre and £10 per acre.[19] But what was equally significant was the contrast between local land prices and the level of wages for agricultural labourers in Barbados. Most agricultural labourers earned less than a shilling a day, and those wages effectively placed ownership of land entirely out of reach of the majority of the emancipated.

This, then, was the situation which confronted the would-be villagers at emancipation and for some time after that fundamental change in their civil status. The plantation was very much a part of their lives and they could do little to escape its tentacles. That point was well summed up in early 1842 in a letter that was written to the governor by the police magistrate for the parish of St Michael:

> Little progress has been made by the labourers in establishing as freeholders, not from any disinclination on their parts to become so, but, circumstanced as our island is, there is little probability of any great number being able to obtain freeholds. The reason is obvious; there is not in the whole island a spot of waste land fit for cultivation; and as the land is principally divided into plantations, the proprietors are not likely to sell off small lots for that purpose; and there being no public lands available, it is plain that freeholds to any extent cannot be established in this country.[20]

This verdict, despite some evidence to the contrary, was to be repeated in the governors' comments on the Barbados Annual Reports in 1848 and 1858. For both governors "the general occupation and high value of land" operated as "obstacles" to the development of villages; and they declared that "the labourers remain on the estates, not because they like the tenure, but because the scarcity and high price of land place freeholds [the bases of free villages] beyond their reach".[21] Therefore, the would-be villager had, for the most part, to rely on *misfortunes* in the plantation-based sugar industry, on bequests from grateful planters, on a few land speculators and on a species of negotiation with planters which was always likely to produce some satisfying results, particularly in any context where planters competed for access to additional labour resources.

This, despite the official near-silence, was what transpired in the century after emancipation. Free Villages were gradually established partly because, first of all, falling prices for cane sugar so increased the debt burden of some planters that a few of them sought to find some relief through the partial subdivision of some small plantations, and mainly because, later on, remittances stimulated the subdivision of larger plantations. Three phases might be identified. The first free villages span the first generation of the emancipated, which also coincided with Peter

Chapman's career as a land speculator that ended in the 1860s, when almost seventy free villages were created as a result of self-help and bequests. The second phase, lasting until the early years of the twentieth century, was in some respects an extension of the first because the same transfer agencies were apparently in play, but it might be suggested that the two hundred-plus villages that were added to the pool were mainly the result of the deepening debt crisis that several planters were encountering. The third phase, beginning when remittances flooded the country after 1907, saw a subdivision of sizeable plantations, which was the necessary precondition for both an increase in the number of free villages and an extension of the existing ones.

THREE
The First Free Villages

Free villages began to be established within the first three decades of slave emancipation, or in the period that roughly coincides with the career of the land speculator, Peter Chapman. Those villages, about seventy in number (table 3.1), containing over seven hundred holdings that occupied more than one thousand acres, could be found all across the island. The greatest concentration apparently occurred in the southern portion of the island: in the parish of St Michael which accommodated the capital town; in the parish of Christ Church which might be called suburban; in St Philip, the largest parish; and in the parish of St George, where the main land speculator, Peter Chapman, was especially active. But it must be noted that the statistics, derived mainly from wills, deeds and one parish rate book, are probably an under-estimate because, for this phase of the free village development, the parish rate books, the official lists of land taxpayers, which are the best sources for the existence of small landowners, survive for only one parish, St Michael for 1852. Therefore, the estimates of the number of free villages and of the holdings in ten of the eleven parishes are based on the somewhat patchy record that exists in the surviving deeds and wills. However, that available evidence demonstrates that, despite the huge constraints that were imposed by limited land space and the planters' declared policies, some free village development did occur even in those early post-slavery years; and this was therefore a remarkable achievement by the newly emancipated people which has not been noticed by historians.

However, it must be emphasized that each cluster of houses (or the smallholdings) did not in general occupy much land space. Aside from the farming lots that were established, for example, at Rock Hall and Bridgefield in St Thomas, at Roberts and at the Farm in St Michael and at Good Intent, Airy Hill, and Workmans in St George, it would appear that, in general, the freed people secured holdings that each was less than one acre in size.

Map 3.1: The First Free Villages

This can be seen most clearly, for obvious reasons, in what is recorded in the rate book for St Michael. At Belle Gully, five of the seven holdings were less than one acre in extent; at Near Collymore Rock, seven of the eleven holdings were less than on acre in size; at Codrington Hill, ten of the eighteen lots were half acre or less; at Two Mile Hill, five of the ten holdings were half an acre in size, while four were a quarter of an acre in extent; and in the district (extended village) of Black Rock, where the range in the size of holding was widest, about thirty-six of the eighty-five holdings that were five acres or under in size were less than an acre in extent.[1]

Further, it must also be noted that free village development did not manifest itself to any extent in those areas where the plantation was most dominant. In other words, free village development (and small-scale landholding) could hardly be found on soils that the geographers described as located Below the Second High Cliff, Above the Second High Cliff and in the St George Valley. Therefore, in general, free village development could not be found in the fertile regions of the parishes of St George, St Thomas and St John. Rather, the free villages were for the most part located on the marginal lands of small properties, on the hillsides, in the gullies and rough pastures that abounded on the land that was located Below the First High Cliff and on the Christ Church Ridge, mainly on the shallow black soils in the parishes of Christ Church and St Michael.

Table 3.1: Location, Estimated Number, Type and Size of the First Free Villages

Parish	Villages	Bequest	Self-help	Holdings	Acreage
Christ Church	18	9	9	141	213 0 00
St Michael	13	1	12	201	245 1 00
St Philip	8	4	4	78	151 1 00
St George	7	---	7	122	190 2 00
St Thomas	5	1	4	67	72 3 00
St Andrew	5	3	2	33	50 2 00
St Lucy	4	4	2	24	41 1 00
St James	3	---	3	30	30 0 00
St John	3	1	2	23	16 2 00
St Joseph	2	1	1	15	10 0 00
St Peter	1	1		6	10 0 00
TOTAL	**69**	**25**	**46**	**740**	**c. 1,031**

Sources: *Deeds, Wills, 1852 St Michael Rate Book*

In addition, internal migration was a factor. Some of the emancipated people, those who could afford it, trekked to Bridgetown and its environs. Though it was noticeable that the traffic increased later, the probability remained that this migration might have been a factor in the location of some of the sites of early free village development. Therefore, the foundation of Black Rock, Codrington Hill, Hothersal Turning, Station Hill, My Lords Hill, St Barnabas and Dayrells Road did almost certainly gain some of its impetus from this migration.

Most important, however, from the perspective of policymakers, both at home and in London, this limited secession from residence on plantation land had no discernible or prolonged effect on the supply of labour to the sugar plantations; and this probably explains why so little official attention was devoted to it. Part of the reason for the negligible impact on the plantations' labour supply was that most of the villagers were still in the geographical ambit of the plantations where they had spent their lives and buried their dead. But the more important point was that, unlike their fellows in Jamaica or in Guyana, the Barbadian emancipated people needed the plantation for their own survival. Put simply, few employment alternatives existed outside of the plantation, and in any case most of the emancipated possessed only farming skills. But given the small extent of land that was eventually acquired by them, it was evident that there existed no possibility that the vast majority of the villagers could substitute own-account farming for regular plantation labour. Therefore, if these people were to survive in Barbados, then plantation labour was their only recourse, which meant that the plantation's ambit was not merely geographical; it was mainly economic. The plantation was where most of the villagers worked, most likely as "strangers",[2] but it was in the villages where they lived, and the nearest plantation was often the name of the village and their postal address.

Land Transfer Agencies

Land for this early free village development was obtained in a variety of ways. But, at the outset, what must be noticed is what was not in place. There were no land settlement schemes; indeed, those who made the local decisions were those who had a stake in frustrating free village development; and the Colonial Office staff was only concerned with whether the contract laws could be construed as means to prolong slavery. There was no need to establish proprietary villages, as was the limited practice in Guyana, Trinidad and Jamaica because potential labourers were in abundance. There was no church/missionary sponsorship, as in Jamaica, which aimed to ensure that the emancipated had both a measure of independence of the plantations and a presence in additional or enlarged congregations for the mission churches.[3] In this regard, the most that could be said was that some Barbadian villages did grow up around Anglican and Methodist churches; and therefore it can be suggested that individual parsons, for example, those at St Barnabas in St Michael, at St Jude's in St George and at St Martin's and at Ebenezer in St Philip, did little to obstruct village development around their churches and chapels. However, those parsons would most likely have encouraged their congregations to accept whatever terms the planters were offering. Finally, unlike Guyana, there was limited evidence of communal action; but the emancipated in Barbados did not face the environmental challenges encountered in Guyana, nor did many of them, given the small size of their provision grounds or gardens, possess the means to acquire land on a cooperative basis.[4]

Bequest Villages

Free villages were established, as indicated in table 3.2, as a result of bequests of land and especially by the employment of a variety of self-help strategies. Those bequest villages will be examined first, not because these were the first free villages to be established, but because bequests were fairly common during slavery when masters did manumit a few of the enslaved and did give them small portions of land to secure that manumission; and therefore, the planters possessed potent sources of paternalism. Now, in emancipation, bequests of land were almost as potent because these could guarantee the means to actualize freedom from slavery or semi-slavery. Therefore, it was perhaps not surprising that some bequests of land, essentially relics from slavery, featured prominently in the establishment of free villages during the first phase.

However, before any of those villages are identified, it might be necessary to clarify how the term is employed. While it is readily accepted that a bequest was the act of a testator in making a gift by a will or similar document to another individual, it is suggested that at least three relevant types of bequest of land could be detected. First was the in-family (legitimate family) type, which could lead to what have been termed family villages. Next there was the *outside family* type which was used to reward paramours and favourite servants *and* to discharge paternal responsibility for *outside* children, and might also lead to the creation of family villages. Finally, there was the general bequest type which rewarded *all* adult servants. Therefore, it is important to recognize that, in post-slavery, all types of bequests of land did possess the potential to advance certain social processes.

About fourteen or fifteen villages, mainly located in the parishes of Christ Church and St Philip, were the result of the first type of bequest. Those villages, especially Douglin Village (in the parish of St Andrew), Cox Road (in the parish of Christ Church), and Nursery (in the parish of St Philip), could more properly be denominated family villages because those villages carried the names of the testators and might represent, in their formation, the consequences of family entail. It must be emphasized, however, that these so-called family villages, at least in their formation, cannot be equated to the consequences of family land tenure which have been discussed by Edith Clarke, M.G. Smith, Sidney Greenfield and Jean Besson.[5] This is not to say that family land tenure did not exist, but oral history would have to confirm its existence. In the instant cases, the formation of these Barbadian *family* villages was based on the written record, but it is possible that continuing land-ownership in some of the villages could have been based on an informal process.

This is entirely probable when the contents of the will of John Christopher Douglin (of the parish of St Andrew), written in September 1852, are examined. He mandated that his three acres and three-quarters were to be divided as follows: one acre to a son; one acre to daughter; one acre to his brother; and the remaining three-quarters of an acre was to be equally divided between a son and daughter who were apparently *outside* children. This was where the family entail provision was written:

> I also order that the above-said three-quarters of an acre just bequeathed to Benjamin and Mimbo Jane must not be sold out of the family should a dissatisfaction take place so that either of them might like to sell; they must give my son Philip Henry the refusal of the purchase of it, and so on if he does not make purchase of it, the family members must have the refusal.[6]

The Douglin Village owed at least its consolidation to Christopher Douglin's instructions.

Three other bequests of this type shed light on the processes of free village formation. The first example was the formation of the Supers village in the parish of St Philip. Technically, its origins are in slavery because Patience Kennedy, a self-described "free mulatto", started the process in her 1794 will. She then decreed that all her land and the enslaved persons at Supers (Suphir Hill) would be at the disposal of her "beloved friend", the enslaved man, Edward Brathwaite, for the benefit of her children; and that, on Edward's death, the property was to be equally divided among her eight children.[7] Edward, for his part, now married after her death and with a second family, decreed in 1831 that ten acres should be given to his five "illegitimate children" who were born of the "body of Patience Kennedy whom I deemed my wife", and that the residue of the estate, possibly another ten acres, should be equally divided among the eleven children that his wife, Margaret Brathwaite, had borne him.[8] To complete the round of bequests, Moses, one of Edward's sons, in 1854 left his four acres and buildings to his eight children; and another son, Samuel, left all his property in his 1868 will to his wife and seven children.[9] Those bequests clearly transformed Supers into a medium-sized village by the 1860s.

Other examples of this type of bequest demonstrated strenuous efforts to create family enclaves. At Greenidges (or Second Step) in the parish of St Lucy, William Johnson Bowen, who owned about sixteen acres, directed in his will of April 1847 that five one-acre lots should be given to four children and a grandson, while the residue of his property, probably six acres and a house, went to his eldest son. However, the heirs decided on an equal division of all the land, and within a year, one of the lots was being sold outside of the family with the approval of the family.[10] In this way, the village of Greenidges was formed. Similarly, at least in intention, were James Sealy's 1857 directions as to the future of his Bright Hill plantation in the parish of Christ Church. That property was to be divided among his five children; the survivors would share the portion of whichever heir died without lawful issue; and the sugar works and distillery should be maintained for three years after his death "at the joint expense of every individual who is to benefit one inch from my land".[11]

Much more of the same can be detected at The Nursery in the parish of St Philip. In 1853, William John Nurse, the owner of about forty-five acres, declared apparently stringent provisions of entail: the bulk of his estate should be "kept together and remain undivided" until all his children reached twenty-one; the property was then to be "equally" divided among eight children and a grandchild; all the shares of the land, except the grandchild's, were to be for life and to be inherited by "lawful issue" of those heirs; if there was no lawful issue, then the share(s) would revert to the surviving heirs for equal division; and on death of heirs' children, their estate was to be divided among their lawful issue.[12] However, by 1875, when the division of the property had already been completed, The Nursery could be regarded as an extended village. While fifteen lots covering forty-one acres could be identified at The Nursery proper, another twenty nine lots, located "Near Nursery" and covering forty-two acres, can also be identified. At the same time, the five-acre lots of five members of the Nurse clan can also be identified, but it was also evident that clustering had taken place, and this was demonstrated by the presence of seventeen owners of lots that were less than one acre in extent.[13] Therefore, in spite of William John Nurse's instructions, the village of The Nursery did emerge as less than a family village; the division of the original property had acted as a magnet for would-be villagers.

Table 3.2: Holdings at The Nursery by 1875

less than one acre	17
1–3 acres	12
3 and less than 5 acres	13
5 acres and over	2

Source: 1875 Rate Book for parish of St Philip

The second type of bequest of land was intended, not so much to create family villages, as to reward retainers and to acknowledge parental responsibilities. In this context, perhaps notice should first be taken of the partial dismemberment of the Harmony Hall property in the parish of Christ Church which led to the consolidation of Bath Village and to the formation of St Lawrence and of Paradise Village. William Malloney Price had owned this sixty-six-acre property, and in his 1808 will he gave to Quaco Price, "my negro boy", his manumission, an annuity, a house and five acres.[14] Quaco, in turn, sold two and a half acres, but decreed in his 1823 will that, after his death, his wife should receive only four dollars while two acres should be given to Mary Catherine Blair, a "free black woman".[15] Then, in 1848/49, Sarah Price, William Malloney Price's widow, completed the property's partial dismemberment. She made gifts of eleven acres to five family members, and then she directed in her 1849 will that another six acres, mainly in half-acre lots, should be given to thirteen individuals who were probably her husband's *outside* children. Those various bequests, particularly Sarah Price's, obviously led to free village formation.[16]

A roughly similar path can be seen in the formation of Sarjeants Village, also in the parish of Christ Church (though the village is technically an early village). Robert Hudgwell Batson, in his will of January 1833, bequeathed Greenidges, a place of twenty-nine and a half acres, to twelve free coloured people and four enslaved persons. The free coloured people were his three paramours and their children, while the four enslaved persons, who were also to be manumitted, were, judging by their surnames, also his children. But the important points were that: as early as 1841–43, at least one of the legatees sold off portions of her bequest; throughout the late 1840s and into the 1850s, there was some evidence of subdivision of the original legacies; and in 1847, one of the original heirs was dividing her share among seven children.[17]

Those features were shared by the remaining ten or twelve free villages, formed by this type of bequest, that were to be mainly found in the parishes of St Andrew and Christ Church. However, the one which captured attention was the aptly named Bequest Village in the parish of St Philip. This village, as far as can be determined from the record, was formed as a result of three bequests of land that, between 1844 and 1860, mainly came out the estates of the infamous Samuel Hall Lord and of James William Streate. While Samuel Hall Lord's will (1844) mentioned two bequests of two-acre lots, it seems fairly evident that his daughter, Elizabeth Sarsfield Lord, did act on his behalf in 1851 in the distribution of at least twenty acres to fifteen individuals who were her father's paramours, their children and his favourite retainers. Moreover, in 1860, Streate's bequest of three *places* (Airy Hill, Little Hope and The Risk) to four children and grandchildren added twenty-three acres to whatever acreage the village already encompassed.[18]

The third type of bequest of land (to all the enslaved adults) did produce two villages, Gibbons Boggs and Pilgrim Road/Pilgrim Place, in the parish of Christ Church. From the record, those villages were the only attempts made by a planter to provide the formerly enslaved population with security of tenure on portions of plantation land; and therefore, these might be favourably compared with Proprietary Villages in other Caribbean countries, even although the motives for the creation of the Barbadian villages seemed to differ from the Guianese versions. Presumably, as a consequence of his recent conversion to Methodism, William Reece, the owner of Pilgrim Place and Gibbons, two medium-sized plantations, did direct in 1835 that each adult "Negro" on his plantations should receive half an acre of his land at the end the apprenticeship (then expected to expire at the end of July 1840); and he specified the (hilly) locations of the gift. Moreover, his declared motive for this unique action was a recognition of common humanity: the gift was intended "to secure homes to these people upon both Estates in considering the working days we have had together".[19] But, unfortunately for the labourers and for the size of early free village development, the gift's potential was never fully realized because Reece's wishes were narrowly construed by the executors of his will. They did lay off eighty-six and a half acres on the two plantations to accommodate Reece's wishes, but they distributed that land on a life tenancy basis, and then, presumably acting on behalf of the new owners of the plantations, they apparently resumed possession of all the land that had not been purchased outright by the beneficiaries or their heirs.[20] Therefore, while the traces of what would have been very substantial free villages at the two locations can be found in 1847, when seventeen men owned one-acre lots at "Pilgrim" and thirteen men owned similarly sized lots at Gibbons, there is no clear trace of the development of the villages.[21] Those villages were not classified as "principal" villages in 1885, and it is therefore impossible to say what precise contribution to the village pool that Reece's gift of land did make. But if the executors of Reece's will did act in laying off the land as soon as the apprenticeship was terminated, then there is a case for concluding that Pilgrim Road/Pilgrim Place and Gibbons Boggs were the earliest free villages in Barbados.

Table 3.3: Table of Estimated Number and Size of Bequest Villages

	Number	Holdings	Acreage
Christ Church	9	79	114
St Philip	4	50	93
St Andrew	3	15	31
St Lucy	2	14	31
St Michael	1	15	15
St Peter	1	6	10
St Joseph	1	5	5
St John	1	10	2
St Thomas	1	5	6
Total	23	199	307

Sources: *Wills and deeds in Barbados Department of Archives*

However, it must be reiterated that the formation of free villages was seldom, if ever, the reason why bequests of small or large portions of land were made, even if those bequests did promote free village development. What seems clear is that the division of land that was contained in a bequest of land did create some opportunities for the formation of extended villages. First, that subdivision could be said to be an early stage of village formation because the existence of undivided blocks of land was obviously a hindrance to smallhold land possession. Second, that subdivision inside a family unit could and did stimulate sales outside of the original family units because it could promote a species of small-scale land speculation and therefore facilitate the presence of outsiders. This point was of particular importance because the available evidence suggested that white persons constituted the vast majority of those who made bequests of land. Therefore, *buy land* or *buy ground* came into the possession of the emancipated when the division of the bequeathed properties made real the possibility of landownership outside of a family unit. That process seemed to have been repeated at all the sites that featured bequests of land that was subsequently divided.

Self-help Activities

The establishment of the majority of the free villages that were identified did seem to be the result of some sort of self-help action by the recently emancipated. Such action involved a limited amount of communal action, some participation in land speculation and mainly "private treaty" arrangements which were the results of a species of negotiation with planters and other landowners.

Communal Action

Communal action, it must be said, was not often recorded, but the few examples of such action should be noticed because these underline the existence of a sustained effort by the emancipated to acquire residences which could be occupied without a legal condition to labour for particular employers. Therefore, the surviving evidence of the formation of Bridgefield and of Redmans Village, both in the parish of St Thomas, and of Endeavour/Orange Hill in the parish of St James, must command attention. At those sites, it seemed evident that some of the emancipated, like their counterparts in British Guiana, were willing to employ almost any means to acquire some land and therefore control to some extent the disposal of their labour.

The largest communal venture apparently occurred at Bridgefield. Nineteen individuals, who were some of the beneficiaries of the cash bequest that had been made in October 1821 by Reynold Alleyne Ellcock (but distributed in 1840), pooled their resources and under the leadership of William Turpin and Callop (Caleb) Dayrell and acquired nearly twelve acres which had been part of the Rugby or Social Hall plantation. Those individuals, formerly enslaved on the Mt. Wilton plantation in the same parish of St Thomas, had then divided the land into twelve lots, varying from half an acre to two and a half acres, which they bought at a previously agreed price from Turpin and Dayrell.[22] As a direct result, the village Bridgefield was established in January of 1841.

At Redmans Village, the base for its foundation was laid in 1845. It was then that Richard Edey, a mason, led a seven-man cooperative which bought two pieces of land from the Provost Marshal totalling almost five acres, and then divided the land among themselves. Consolidation of the existence of the village came in 1851 when family property of fifteen acres was distributed in five equal shares. At Endeavour/Orange Hill in the parish of St James, Robert Jackman's sale of four quarter-acre lots in 1854 out of a two-acre property was apparently done on a cooperative basis and led to the consolidation of the twin villages.[23] Perhaps there were other examples of cooperative action, but the records of these are the only ones that seemed to have survived.

Land Speculation

Most of the villages were apparently established through some form of land speculation. The point has to be stated tentatively because direct evidence of the influence of this factor has been established in the formation of about fifteen of the sixty-nine free villages, and therefore a measure of speculation must surround the establishment of about half of the villages in the self-help category. But, first, it must be made clear how the term "speculation" is employed in this context. It is used, not in the sense of sellers hawking the sale of an available commodity (and therefore placing at risk their original investments), but as the act of individuals who recognize a ready market or targets of opportunity and rush in to reap the guaranteed profits. Therefore, given the limited amount of land that was available for sale in small portions, land speculation may not have been perennial activity.

Except in the case of one man, Peter Chapman, this activity seemed to have featured men who were essentially one-off operators. At least six land *speculators* can so far be positively identified. But, while five of them did not make the selling of land their main or only business, they may be classed as land speculators because, while, in general, they did not buy land in order to sell it, they did sell land, their own land, in small lots at way above the market price for land that was being sold as entire plantations. These men therefore have to be distinguished from

Peter Chapman, who was in the business for more than thirty years and bought and sold land in four parishes. Those five other men can therefore be termed the one-off land speculators.

The Rock Hall village in the parish of St Thomas, the sister village of Bridgefield, seems to have been the first village that was formed as a result of one-off land speculation. This village, established between September 1840 and December 1844, was essentially the result of a combination of the means to buy small portions of land and the availability of such land. The means were the payment in July 1840 of a bequest of £85 to eighty-three legatees on the Mount Wilton plantation. This sum of money represented the simple accumulation of the £5 annuity that Reynold Alleyne Ellcock had bequeathed in October 1821 to "each labouring adult" among the "Negroes" on his Mount Wilton plantation as a reward for "their uniform good conduct...more particularly in the Insurrection" (the 1816 slave revolt). The available land was a section of the Farm Plantation, which now embraced some of the lands of the dismembered Rock Hall Plantation. This land had become available because Joseph Gibbs Bayley, the owner of Ridgeway and Farm plantations, recognizing in the payment of the bequest an opportunity both "to escape pecuniary difficulties" and to finance a career change (from planter to journalist), placed about forty acres of this land of variable quality on the market. It seems clear that Bayley's actions, from organizing the land survey and pricing the lots at £70 per acre to completing the legal formalities, were motivated by news of the impending payment of the bequest.[24]

At least thirty of the recipients of the Ellcock Bequest bought lots at Rock Hall and therefore participated in its foundation as a free village. But it must be emphasized that this village cannot be properly denoted a bequest village because while the Ellcock Bequest did enable labourers to purchase the land which constituted the village, that bequest did not mandate how the cash should be expended. In other words, the legatees had choice in how to spend the cash, and a minority of them did evidently exploit that opportunity. But it was the exercise of choice in a specific manner by some of them that explains why a majority of the recipients of the Ellcock Bequest founded the villages of Rock Hall and Bridgefield.

At the same time, it must be noticed how the Rock Hall village fitted into the parameters of Barbadian free village development. First, it provided what William Knibb had called a "refuge" or an "asylum". That is, the emancipated were freed from those legal requirements which residence in a plantation tenantry did entail: they were now free to take their labour to the best market, or become self-employed or partly self-employed. Second, the quantity and quality of the available land did not provide much opportunity for the villagers to become full-time small farmers. The lots seldom exceeded an acre in size, and in any case the legatees could not afford more than one lot, and the quality of the soil was generally poor. Most of the land was slope, with gradients of five to twelve inches, and the depth of the soil varied from twelve to over twenty inches. Those soil conditions probably explained why the Rock Hall plantation had failed: knowledgeable planters declared that the lands were "considered generally bad" and were "proverbial for not yielding any return".

However, the formation of this village was significant for several reasons. First, it apparently became a sort of model that Peter Chapman replicated in the various farming lots that he sold between 1846 and 1856. This was perhaps not much of a surprise because Chapman was Bayley's assistant at Rock Hall: he witnessed some of the deeds and no doubt invested the sales with the requisite legal rigour. Second, the Rock Hall village provided an early glimpse of the political potential that villagers could employ in the days of property qualification for the exercise of the franchise. At least twelve of these new villagers were participants in the Controverted Election of 1849. They had joined Samuel Jackman Prescod's Liberal Party, a rainbow coalition, which was mobilizing its members to secure an extension of the franchise and the election of "honest and intelligent men" who would "promote the interests of the general community". To this end, Prescod's party, clearly realizing that the villagers might qualify for the £20 franchise, mounted a voter registration campaign in the free villages in the parishes of St Thomas and St Michael in order to win seats in the 1848 election. That effort produced the anticipated results: the number of qualified voters in St Thomas almost doubled; and twenty-one of those registered voters, including twelve from Rock Hall, requested two Liberal Party candidates to carry the party's flag into the election against the sitting members, Dr James Sarsfield Bascom and John Grant, who were identified with the Conservative interest.

Rock Hall voters therefore played a central role in the both the election campaign and its eventual result. The extended campaign, as expected, was the occasion for the ventilation of invective and the creation of a mini-political crisis. The *Barbadian* newspaper deplored the "ultra-radicalism" which was bringing "the scum to the surface", lamented the fact that persons of the "baser sort" were attempting "to deprive the island of every respectable man who had a seat in the Assembly", and published a letter which lambasted the "low radicals" who were exploiting "poor deluded simpletons" who were "blockheads owning half an acre or three quarters". The opposition, the *Liberal*, Prescod's newspaper, reported that Dr Bascom had said: "do you suppose that a handful of Niggers and Mulattoes can manage me?" Moreover, it deplored the "rascality" of the *Barbadian*, dismissed "the peculiar gentility of the parish", and argued that the time had come to give the doctor "rest".[25]

The impact of the Rock Hall (and other village) voters on the elections was immense. In the general election, Haynes Bayley, one of the Liberal Party's candidates, topped the polls in the double member constituency, scoring one more vote than the sitting members. Because this meant that one of the sitting members would lose his seat, the Conservatives immediately challenged the results, alleging that twelve voters, including nine from Rock Hall, were not qualified to vote. This, as was the custom, prompted the House of Assembly to closely investigate the franchise qualifications of five of the voters, four of whom came from Rock Hall. In the event, it ruled that only one of Haynes Bayley's votes was "bad", which had the effect of creating a three-way tie at the top of the poll, thereby necessitating a by-election. But though the situation remained tense, the Conservatives, already bruised in the campaign, did not participate in the by-election, thereby handing victory to the party of the so-called "blockheads".

The third reason why the Rock Hall village was significant was that its early history also provided evidence that could be deemed sociological. This could be seen in the building of the additional houses on some holdings in the village in order to provide shelter for kin who had lived in the plantation tenantry, and this was most evident in the fragmentation of the original lots that was decreed in the wills of some of the original owners. For example, an examination of eight wills revealed that it was likely that some landowners at Rock Hall divided their holdings among children and grandchildren, to the extent that the original lots became a series of virtual house-spots. This had two obvious consequences. First, few Rock Hall villagers were now qualified to exercise the franchise: by 1867 only four of them were registered voters, and by 1875, there were merely nine qualified voters when at least twenty could be counted in the 1840s. Therefore, the 1848/49 scenario was unlikely to be repeated.

Second, subdivision of the original holdings could be said to impede legatees' social and economic advance. While it was entirely possible that many of the original lots did contain potential for economic and social advance, the creation of the virtual house-spots by the original owners did deprive the new owners of occupational options and the possibility of consequential social advance. Therefore, it can be suggested that the actions of the original landowners, especially in the fragmentation of their lots, which was repeated in other villages, meant that, at this stage, the founders of free villages were elevating family cohesion and escape from the plantation tenantry over most economic and political considerations.

Similar information is unfortunately not available about the other villages in which the one-off speculators participated. Therefore, the limited information can be quickly presented in a chronological fashion. Vauxhall village in the parish of Christ Church was formed between 1842 and 1845 as a result the sale of small lots by James Sullivan, a small planter. This was in every sense a small operation. The lots came out of a ten-acre property that Sullivan owned; the eleven lots that were carved out of it totalled less than six acres in extent; and sale of nine of the eleven lots took place by 1849. But it might be noticed that Sullivan charged £100 per acre, thereby ratifying his status as a land speculator.[26]

Table 3.4: Estimates of the Number and Size of Speculators' Villages

	Villages	Size (Acres)
Peter Chapman	9	300
Joseph Bayley	1	40
Samuel James Mayers	1	19
James Browne Mapp	1	13
Robert Thomas Outram	1	12
James Sullivan	1	5
Totals	**14**	**389**

The Cave Hill/Rock Dundo village in the parish of St Michael was established partly as a result of sales of lots by Samuel James Mayers in 1847. Little is known about him, but presumably he was a planter. He had acquired the fifty-four-acre Rock Dundo Plantation, and he promptly sold off a third of it at about £50 per acre. This was a low price, perhaps determined by its hilly location, and it is possible that he was attempting to recover a portion of the plantation's purchase price of about £40 per acre. Most of all, he may have wanted access to some of the cash that Peter Chapman, the one professional land speculator, was busily collecting from land sales in the vicinity.[27] Waverley Cot in the parish of St George was the result of sales by Robert Thomas Outram in 1851–54. This resident of the parish of St Philip sold twelve acres in eight lots of the Murrays *place* that he had acquired under a mortgage, and he charged the comparatively low price of £52 per acre.[28] Cherry Grove in the parish of St John owed its formation in 1853 to sales by James Brown Mapp. This non-white, who was described as mechanic and a mason, was clearly climbing the social ladder, and he had earned the honorific of "esquire" by 1853. He bought the thirteen-and-a-half-acre Cherry Grove *place* in 1848, and in 1853, no doubt recognizing an opportunity for profit-taking, he sold the property in eight lots to eight labourers. He can be termed a land speculator because he charged £125 an acre for each acre, which represented a profit of £40 on every acre that he sold.[29]

However, special attention should be paid to seven of the nine free villages created as a result of the efforts of Peter Chapman, the lone professional land speculator. Those villages represented the clearest evidence of free village development.[30] The first of those villages, one of the "farming lots", was formed in the parish of St Michael at the fourteen-acre property, Roberts Tenantry, sometimes referred to as "Near Neils". In August 1846, Chapman sold seven lots (one had already been sold by his sisters) that varied in size from half an acre to three acres, and the selling price ranged from £62 to £85 per acre. Other Chapman villages in the same parish included the Farm. At that site, forty-three acres were subdivided under Chapman's direction during 1853, and the one- and two-acre lots, numbering about thirty, fetched prices that ranged from £62 to £80 per acre. Similarly, at Content/Bermuda Land, Chapman figured during 1851–52 in the sale of a twenty-three-acre property in eight lots that fetched prices of as much as £68 per acre.

Chapman was especially active in the parish of St George. At Good Intent/Cane Hill, Chapman during 1847 subdivided the fourteen acres that he had bought in a judicial sale. He sold the nine lots, ranging in size from half an acre to two acres, for £58 per acre, netting a profit of 100 per cent. At Airy Hill, he subdivided the land that he had bought in two parcels in 1853 and 1866. He sold off twenty-nine lots that varied in size between one and three acres at prices that ranged between £66 and £125 per acre. In 1854, he bought Campion/Campaign Castle and divided the ten-acre property into nine lots. His activities climaxed in 1856 when he bought Workmans Land, the hilly section of the Walkers plantation. He paid £3,500 for 102 acres, and he laid out at least fifty-six lots that were mainly between one acre and two acres in size, and he sold these at a median price of £83 per acre.

Three features of these *Chapman* villages command attention. First, he deliberately offered the opportunity to form villages over a period of twenty years, 1846–67, and thereby catered to an expressed need. Thus, it would appear that Chapman, the lawyer, actually sought out property that his other professional activities told him was likely to be on sale; that he might even have engineered some of the sales himself; and that he proceeded to service a need that was being expressed all around him. But, most of all, as a true professional, he saw that large profits could be made from the servicing of that need, and he ensured that those profits were forthcoming by imposing large mark-ups on whatever price he had paid for the land that he subsequently subdivided. That mark-up was never less than 50 per cent, and it often exceeded 200 per cent, but that did not prevent him from tightly binding most of his clients to their legal obligations in respect of sales of lots. However, the obvious points persist: Chapman was never short of buyers, and the deeds confirm that a typical purchaser of a lot was a "labourer".

The second reason why attention should be paid to these free villages was their size in comparison with most of the other village sites. These *Chapman* villages were, in general, larger than most of the self-help villages, both in terms of overall acreage and in terms of the size of the individual lots. Most of the holdings in the other self-help villages seemed to range between a quarter and a half of an acre, but in the *Chapman* villages the size of the holding was generally at least one acre. Equally impressive was the overall size of the villages, particularly at the Farm, at Airy Hill, and at Workmans. Only Rock Hall was of comparable size to the Farm and to Airy Hill, and it should be noted that special circumstances account for the size of the Rock Hall village. But, in any case, Workmans might be placed in a separate category from all these first phase free villages because it was comfortably the largest piece of plantation land that was made available for subdivision. Perhaps it was its location on a hillside, perhaps it was the adverse pecuniary circumstances of the original owners, perhaps it was persistence of the land speculator. But whatever the reasons, single or in a combination, portions of this large block of land could now be purchased by would-be villagers on an instalment plan. Clearly, at least in this first phase, these villages contained farming lots.

The third reason why these villages were noteworthy was because the villages embedded certain procedures for village formation. Those procedures were the consequences of the practices of payment by instalment and of the legal safeguarding of the speculator's investment, and these could be said to both promote and hinder village formation. In the first place, village formation was promoted because Chapman, along with his first business partner, Dr William John King, brought the purchase of a lot within the reach of some of the emancipated people through payment for their lots on the instalment principle or "accommodating terms", as they described them. This involved, they said as early as 1839, the down payment of "a small part of purchase money", and a legally binding contract to pay the balance over "several years". On the one hand, this could be considered to be very timely because it would attract business from potential clients, the land-hungry emancipated, who could not pay upfront Chapman's prices for land on the low wages that they were receiving. Therefore, it did appear to be a win-win all around: the land speculators' business would be boosted; some of the blacks would acquire land; and Chapman would win plaudits from influential members of the black community, like Samuel Jackman Prescod and J.L. Wilkinson.

On the other hand, however, it could be said that the devil was in the legal details. Chapman so tightly secured his investment that non-compliance by a purchaser of a lot meant expulsion from a village project and the loss of the down payment and instalments. This can be easily deduced from Chapman's modus operandi: he took a mortgage on each lot that he sold; he crafted a repayment schedule; he charged interest at 6 per cent on outstanding payments; and he asserted a right of re-possession in cases of default. Cases of re-possession did occur, and those cases, when added to the pricing of lots, would suggest that the would-be smallholder/villager may have been the victim of gouging.[31]

Private Treaty Arrangements

Precise information was unfortunately not available for the formation of about one-half of the remainder of self-help villages. First, it would seem that many more one-off land speculators were in the field, and there is some slight evidence that they may have been active at Dayrells Road, at Maxwell Hill, at Rose Hill, and at St Patrick's in the parish of Christ Church, at Dash Valley in the parish of St George and at Brereton in the parish of St Philip. This all seems likely because no official was keeping tabs on what most landowners did, and it followed that several transactions were never recorded. Second, it must be conceded that there might have been traffic among some of the new villagers, particularly among those who were the recipients of sizeable bequests, between individuals who might have seen the advantages of some small trading. Third, and most important, was the manner in which several of the free villages seemed to have been formed. That manner of formation was generally indicated by a postal address that was "Near" or "By" a plantation. This seems to provide a clear clue: the villages so denominated had been formed as results of gifts or sales of small portions of plantation land. This explanation can be offered because, in spite of the articulation of a thesis that resistance by blacks was general in slavery and post-slavery,[32] it seems reasonable to assume that there was a range of relationships, not only between the enslaved and the "master" but also between the planter/employer and the labourer. Therefore, it is likely that some planters, in spite of the anti-village rhetoric, were induced, by one consideration or other, into releasing small portions of their plantations to favourite servants. Moreover, the individual planter, facing an uncertain prospect that was being glimpsed in declining profits from cane sugar during the 1850s and 1860s, was perhaps likely to seek short-term and possibly private advantage, whether or not the objective was worldly. Therefore, it is entirely possible that some free villages were in a sense spawned by the plantation – that free village development received active assistance from some planters.

FOUR
Free Village Expansion

The expansion of free villages during this second phase, roughly 1870 to 1905, was impressive, particularly in terms of the number of free villages. That number more than tripled, but there was apparently not a corresponding increase in the acreage that these villages (and holdings) did occupy. Moreover, all the evidence suggests the settlement intensified in the earlier villages, particularly in the larger villages. The statistics presented in table 4.1 roughly indicate what had transpired in the period between Peter Chapman's retirement from land speculation and the time when inflows of Panama Money dramatically transformed the picture. The number of free villages had topped two hundred, those new villages contained nearly four thousand holdings, and those

Table 4.1: New Free Villages, Approximate Numbers, 1870–1905

Parish	Villages	Bequest	Self-Help	No. of Holdings	Acreage
Christ Church	47	2	45	940	658
St Philip	47	3	44	732	688
St Michael	32	1	31	487	290
St George	28	4	24	551	304
St Lucy	20	4	16	251	166
St Joseph	17	2	15	150	175
St Andrew	10	1	9	194	156
St James	10	....	10	177	105
St John	9	2	7	135	96
St Peter	7	1	6	130	69
St Thomas	6	2	4	52	66
Totals	**233**	**22**	**211**	**3,799**	**2,773**

Source: *Parish Rate Books, wills and deeds in BDA*

holdings occupied about twenty-seven hundred acres of land space. It was the size of this numerical expansion of villages which no doubt impelled G.W. Sisnett, the chairman of the St George Vestry, to tell the Water Supply Commission in 1885 that "as far as can be estimated, these villages contain about two-thirds of the whole population of the parish".[1] While he did not furnish any statistical evidence in support of his assertion, it seemed evident that the increase in the number of free villages, because of its size, was certain to bother officials who, up to that point, had hardly acknowledged the existence of those villages.

Map 4.1: The Increase in Number of Free Villages

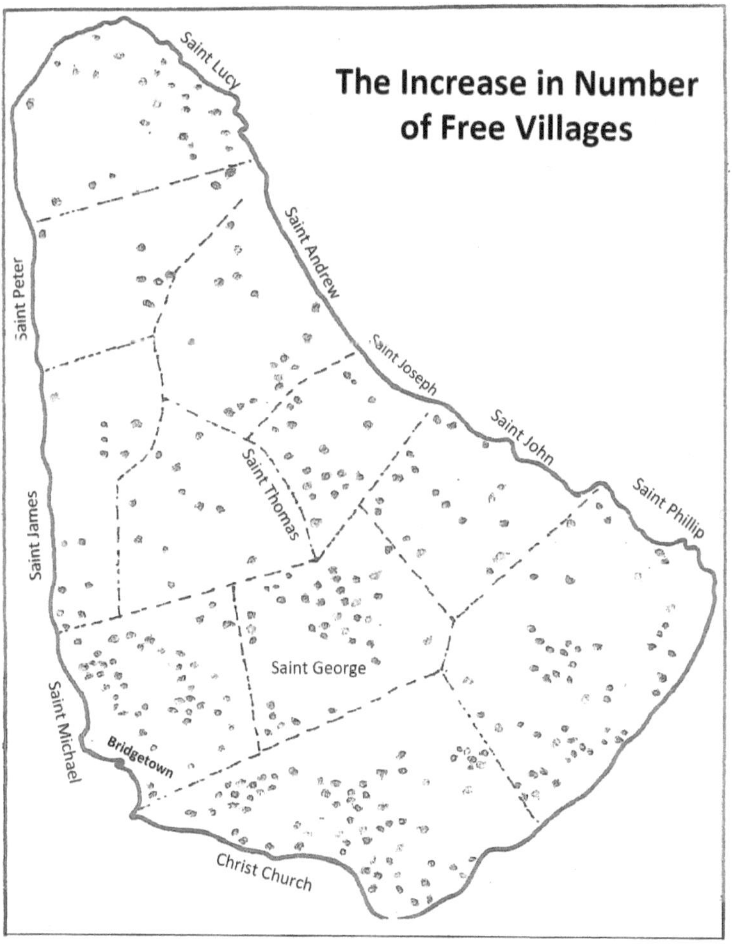

This increase seemed to have mainly occurred in six parishes. On the face of it, it seems as though a larger land area in four of those parishes (St Philip, Christ Church, St Michael, and St George) might explain why those parishes dominated the development, and it is also true that those four parishes contained land that seemed to be available for smallhold land development. St Philip and Christ Church had both extensive seacoast plains and shallow soils; St George possessed some hilly country in the Lowland Plateau; and St Michael was the site of the capital town. But, at the same time, it is probable that the available statistics do not tell the full story. This probability must exist because the parish rate books which, because these are the records of the taxes that were paid by all landowners, are the reliable guide to landowning, cannot be consulted for all the parishes during the specific period. Those relevant records for six of the parishes seem not to have not survived; but as far as possible, some of the features of this development have been recovered from deeds and wills, and this information must therefore do duty for the absent records in any survey of the features of free village development.[2]

Those features were revealed through an examination of the distribution and density of the free villages across the eleven parishes. This was done through the employment of a dual classification (tables 4.1 and 4.2). Parishes were ranked as top-tier: areas of large concentration of free villages or those that possessed more than twenty-five villages in number; middle-tier or average-sized, those that accommodated more than ten but less than twenty-five villages; and bottom-tier parishes, those that were the home to ten or less than ten villages. Then, the probable distribution of holdings (and acreage) in each parish is presented to illustrate the extent to which each parish accommodated small villages (with ten holdings or less), medium-sized villages (with more than ten and up to twenty-five holdings) and large villages (with more than twenty-five holdings).

First in the top tier of parishes was Christ Church. This parish, as it had been the case during the first phase of free village development, led the way in the accommodation of free villages during this second phase. While the quickening pace of village development in the parish of St Philip meant that this parish seemed to be closing in on Christ

Church's lead, both parishes, along with St Michael and St George, easily constituted the parishes with the largest concentrations of villages.

Table 4.2: Distribution of Villages According to Number of Holdings

Parish	Ten or Less Holdings	Eleven to Twenty-five Holdings	Twenty-five Holdings
Christ Church	18	18	11
St Philip	19	19	9
St Michael	15	14	3
St George	5	18	5
St Joseph	12	4	1
St Lucy	12	8	...
St Andrew	4	5	1
St James	2	6	2
St Peter	5	....	2
St John	5	4	....
St Thomas	5	1	....
TOTALS	102	97	34

Source: *Parish Rate Books and deeds in BDA*

But the point to notice with respect to Christ Church was that more than 75 per cent of its forty-seven villages were in the small- and medium-sized categories; it therefore mainly accommodated villages that were relatively small, both in terms of the number holdings and of acreage. This was an important finding because it clearly revealed what was characteristic of all stages of free village development across the island: most of the villagers could only manage to acquire either a quarter or half an acre. Therefore, they remained almost securely in the ambit of the plantation, partly because they were grateful to those planters who had occasionally hived off small portions of their acreage, but mainly because the planation remained the main source of employment and income. However, at the same time, it should be noticed that the parish of Christ Church was also the home of almost one-third of the large villages, though only three, Near Enterprise, Thornbury Hill and Near

Warners, each accommodated more than fifty holdings in 1901. Indeed, it would seem that only Newbury (sixty-seven holdings) in the parish of St George could compete with Near Warners (eighty-five holdings) for the distinction of being the largest village that was formed during this second phase of free village development. But, in any case, all free villages had to yield primacy in the size of village to one other St George village that had been established in the first phase. That village, Workmans, contained as many as 136 holdings in 1893.

The parish of St Philip, along with Christ Church, recorded the largest growth in the number of free villages, accommodating nearly six times as many as had been formed in the first phase (forty-seven as against eight). These new villages, like those in the parish of Christ Church, were mainly in the small and medium categories, and it was perhaps significant that the average size of all holdings was in excess of three-quarters of an acre. Some nine "large" villages existed in the parish, but only one, Blades Hill, was identified as a "principal" village in 1885; and Near Mangrove was the lone village that, according to the parish rate book, accommodated fifty holdings (on thirty-eight acres) in 1901. However, that village in its size bore no real comparison with its neighbour, Foul Bay, an early "Red Leg" village, which in 1901 accommodated more than 130 holdings on 172 acres.

In the parish of St Michael, the pattern of increase and distribution was roughly similar to that in the parishes of Christ Church and St Philip. Some thirty-two new villages were created, and twenty-nine small- and medium-sized villages featured in that number. Only Ramparts among several village clusters was described as a "principal" village in 1885, but Rouen (thirty-four holdings) and Howell Cross Roads (forty-two holdings) could have qualified for that designation by 1901. But it is noticeable that, as might be expected from its suburban location, as many as thirty-six of the forty-two holdings at Howell Cross Roads were less than an acre. The other noticeable feature of those villages was a distinct variation in naming. While the nearest plantation often featured in the names of most villages, here in St Michael there was an increasing usage of a road or gap (Westbury Road, Licorish Gap, Government Hill) to identify village location, and perhaps the suburban setting explained this variation.

The parish of St George rounded out the group of first tier parishes. Here could be found a large increase in number of villages, a dominance of medium-sized villages, and a few interesting names. Eighteen of the twenty-eight new villages could be classified as average-sized, that is, containing between eleven and twenty-five holdings, and the average-sized holding barely exceeded half an acre. Some nine of the free villages in the parish were designated as "principal" villages in 1885, which meant, according to the chairman of the vestry, that each village contained at least five hundred persons. However, the parish rate book for 1893 suggested that, according to taxes collected, the designation of "principal" might have properly belonged to Flat Rock, Old Post Office, Market Hill, Rock Hall or Near Walkers and Newbury because all these villages each possessed in excess of twenty-five holdings. In this context, Newbury stands out because its sixty-seven holdings in 1893 easily made it one of the largest villages that was formed in this second phase. At the same time, it must be noticed that the sixty-seven holdings in that village occupied only thirty-four acres; and it was this distribution of acreage, which could be found in other villages in the parish, that ensured the parish possessed the least amount of land per holding. The names, which had more to do with climate, topography and public function, could be identified as Cole Hole, Flat Rock and Old Post Office.

The parishes of St Lucy and St Joseph constituted the middle tier of parishes, or those parishes which accommodated between eleven and twenty-five villages. In both parishes, the number of small villages far outnumbered all other villages, and though the chairmen of the vestries identified as many as eight free villages among the "principal" villages in 1885, only Braggs Hill in St Joseph apparently contained as many as thirty-seven holdings. Of course, it is probable the deficiencies in the written record explain why Avis (Avice) Town, Benthams, Crab Hill, Graveyard, Nesfield and Rock Hall, all in the parish of St Lucy, as well as Branchberry and St Sylvans in St Joseph, apparently did not contain the number of holdings (and acres) to render those villages as significant foundations. Finally, one should notice that names like Bowling Alley in St Joseph, and Crab Hill, Graveyard and Swampy Town in St Lucy were interesting additions to the lexicon.

The remaining five parishes, St Andrew, St James, St Peter, St John, St Thomas, seemed to represent the bottom tier of parishes, those parishes with the lowest concentration of villages during this phase. The point has to be rendered in tentative fashion because full documentary evidence of free village development in those parishes has not survived; and therefore the estimates of the size of the free villages are necessarily presented in a conservative fashion. Thirty-seven of the forty-two villages were judged to be small- and medium-sized, that is, each of those villages contained holdings that did not exceed twenty-five. The chairmen of the vestries did identify six of these villages, namely Dorants and Mt. All in the parish of St Andrew, and Coach Hill, Gall Hill, Spooner's and Wilson Hill in the parish of St John, as "principal" villages in 1885, but there was strong evidence that five other villages, Belleplaine in St Andrew, Diamond Corner and Mile and Quarter in the parish of St Peter, and Greenwich and Prospect in St James, could be classified as "large" villages by 1905. These villages each seemed to contain more than twenty-five holdings. Of these, perhaps Belleplaine and Mile and Quarter attracted the most attention because these were evidently expanding centres of settlement. Finally, the features of village formation in the parish of St Thomas might be noticed. This parish was almost wholly situated in the red-soil district and on the Upland Plateau, and it therefore possessed some of the island's most fertile soil. Not surprisingly, therefore, it contained the least number (seven) of free villages. Though free village development might have begun in that parish, that fact was most likely the unintended consequence of a charitable gesture that was not influenced by any environmental or ideological considerations.[3] The only other point of significance seemed to be the names of some villages in this category of villages. "Arise" and "Shop Hill" in St Thomas; "Curiosity Village" and "Hermill" in St James; "Lonesome Hill" and "Mile and Quarter" in St Peter; and "Zores" in St John: all these may have been quaint descriptions of particular environments by a few villagers.

Over all, then, this increase in the number of villages significantly modified the island's settlement pattern. The increasing secession from residence in the plantation tenantries or "nigger yard" meant that, by the start of the twentieth century, at least one-third of the island's population lived in the three hundred free villages that had been created. Of course, this also meant that the villagers were near to the plantation. This was inevitably the case, not merely because of the island's small size, but because the plantation's virtual monopoly of land space left little room for land appropriation by the emancipated people and their descendants. This was demonstrated by the fact that, during this phase, the average size of each holding in the villages was far short of one acre, and in fact holdings of half an acre and of a quarter acre in extent were the dominant feature in most villages.

Two issues naturally arise: the range of factors that led to the increase in the number of free villages and the community's response to that increase. At a general level, that increase in the number of villages might have been the result of the interplay of factors which had caused a weakening of the plantation's tight grip on the land space. First, it is suggested that, from the late 1840s, the stability and prospects of the cane sugar economy and plantation society were threatened by crisis and near crisis which, until the end of the century and later, called for frequent adjustments. The Commercial Crisis of 1847 started it all by damaging the planters' credit lines in both England and Barbados, and this was followed by the cholera pandemic which killed about twenty thousand, sparing neither planters nor labourers. Therefore, the planters and merchants, the island's ruling class, were not best equipped to cope with the prospect of the declining incomes which the lowered price and an insecure market for cane sugar would inflict on them when the Free Trade and the Sugar Duties Act took control of British policy. Indeed, some early adjustments did stave off the inevitable, even brought some prosperity, but bounty-fed beet sugar brought near the prospect of virtual ruin.[4] Therefore, by the 1870s and 1880s, the planters, in particular, unless they were partially blinded by notions of aristocracy, obviously had to adjust living styles and expectations and as a consequence adopt short-term survival policies while they mainly courted imperial assistance.

Their local responses, however, did provide an unintended fillip to free village formation. This could be seen in the relaxation of anti-emigration measures, implemented early in the 1860s, which ensured that the prevailing social distress, felt mainly by the working classes, was partially eased by the departure of more than one thousand persons annually. Then came the unintended consequence: the government's action made it possible for remittances to be enjoyed. Though it is obviously impossible to estimate the direct consequences of those remittances on free village formation, it is reasonable to assume that the higher wages which were available in Trinidad and Guyana meant that the relatives who were left behind in Barbados could and did invest the savings that were remitted in land purchase and village formation.[5]

Second, the planters' habitual responses of retrenchment and lower wages did actively promote village formation. This happened because planters' responses prompted an increase in decampment from plantation tenantry residence and a significant rural to urban migration, and this is well indicated by census statistics that showed a growing population in the urban areas of St Michael and in the suburban areas of both St Michael and Christ Church. Put simply, the people who flooded the suburban corridors of those two parishes had to be accommodated. Some of them were seeking opportunities to emigrate, but most of them were clearly hoping that residence near to the capital city would improve their prospects of earning employment. In any case, they needed shelter. Therefore, it is easy to see why villages were formed and the existing villages were extended along the corridors, from the Black Rock district, Green Hill and Codrington Hill to Hothersal Turning and Station Hill, to My Lords Hill and Government Hill, to St Barnabas and Collymore Rock, to Brittons Hill, Dayrells Road and Hastings.

Third, the individual planter responses must be recognized. While the rhetoric of the ruling classes continued to declare that small landholding was deleterious to the health of the economy and the society, it seemed clear that this position was not necessarily reflected in the actions of several planters, probably the smaller planters. Though those planters never expressed a contrary opinion in public, their actions, driven by individual interests, were presumably the main reason why influential individuals kept on repeating the mantra about the dangers of small landholding. The point here is that it was obvious to the society's leaders that village development was taking place, and they constantly warned about it in public. Therefore, it would appear that the would-be villagers/small landowners encountered at this time a dichotomy: influential opinion that was clamouring for their non-existence and, on the other hand, individual planters who, probably for a variety of reasons, were assisting them in breaching the wall of plantation land monopoly.

Bequests

Bequests of land played only a small role in the breaching of that wall. Compared with the first phase when one-third of the new villages were apparently formed as a result of bequests of land, now those bequests apparently featured in the formation of only about 10 per cent of the free villages established during this second phase. This relative disappearance of bequests of land was probably the result of changes in the social order rather than a reduction in charity or benevolence. The simple point may be this: the property holders, mainly planters, no longer in post-slavery had the huge power of patronage that was contained in the right to manumit and also to grant small lots of land with which they had rewarded a few of their enslaved labourers, mainly their concubines and children.

The relevant bequests of land in this second phase therefore detailed various gifts to established family members. Most of the benefactors ignored the English practice of primogeniture by instead stressing an equal division of family property, usually among children, whether these were "reputed" or the products of marriages. Occasionally, gifts of land were made to a "woman", as was the case of John Francis Gill of Durhams in the parish of St Lucy and of Thomas Henry Straughan of Straughan's Village in the parish of St Joseph,[6] but the usual practice was detailed in George Christie's will. His five acres at Windy Hill in the parish of St Thomas (which became the base of Christie's Village) was to be equally divided among a son and two daughters.[7] However, it was George Francis Holder in the parish of St George whose will best summed up what seemed to be the prevailing practice. He wrote that his holding of one and a half acres was to be equally divided among six daughters and two sons. The youngest son was mandated to receive the section "from the Limestone in the back to the Fruit tree in the centre"; the other seven children were slated to divide the remainder of the land; and then came Holder's key directive. "The said land," he wrote, "is not to be sold by none of the children—[it] is to be for seed to seeds".[8]

Land Speculation

Land speculation as a means of land transfer was not as prominent as it had been during the first phase. It is true that attention must be drawn to the activities of one professional land speculator, Charles Joseph Greenidge, but there is no clear evidence that many one-off land speculators did not rake in profits from the land-hungry. It is possible that Robert Doughty Blades at Work Hall in the parish of St Philip, William Clarke of Clarke's Hill, also in the parish of St Philip, John Thomas Ellis at Carrington Village in the parish of St Thomas and Ralph Cyril Murphy at Market Hill in the parish of St George did engage in one-off land speculation, but the jury must remain out until evidence of substantial mark-ups in relation to their assorted land sales can be collected.

This leaves for consideration the activities of the one professional, Charles Joseph Greenidge (1845–1910). In some respects, he can be compared with Peter Chapman. Like Chapman, he was a professional by training, and he too may have seen land speculation as a highly profitable sideline. But there were also some points of difference, indicated especially by the spread of Greenidge's interests. He was also a building contractor/architect, a property developer, an entrepreneur, a trader in plantations and an occasional politician. He may have owned as many as seven or eight plantations at some point, and he lived on plantations, and his land speculation and subdivision seemed to have occurred on three or four of those plantations.[9]

The Ivy, which became a densely populated suburban village in the parish of St Michael, was the first result of his ministrations. In 1888, he bought and then subdivided what was essentially an amalgamation of six small properties, Rouen, O'Neal's, Eastcott, Millington's, Windsor Lodge and Prospect, covering some seventy-four acres. What was remarkable was that he disposed of most of the two-hundred-plus lots that he carved out of the property and simultaneously helped to create both a free village and a middle-class residential subdivision. Therefore, the Ivy comprised two developments: a working-class village set up on tiny lots and a middle-class residential subdivision that was no doubt created as an imitation of what Sam Manning had done at Belleville a short distance away.

No such ambiguity surrounded the subdivision at Greenwich (sixty-eight acres) in the parish of St James, at Newbury (ninety-three acres) and Middleton (forty-three acres) in the parish of St George, and at Cane Garden (122 acres) in the parish of St Andrew. At Greenwich, the village and the large remnants of the plantation shared the site and the name, with the village being much the junior partner. However, at Newbury and Middleton, the situation was seemingly reversed: the villages effectively replaced the plantations. At Cane Garden, the partial conversion to a free village seemed to have occurred after 1905. However, apart from the dismissive comments that A.J. Pile made about the blacks' demand for land being adequately satisfied by the subdivision of two small plantations,[10] the formation of those villages apparently made no apparent impact on the planters' consciousness and certainly did not fully meet blacks' expectations.

Private Treaty Arrangements

The bulk of the free villages was formed, it would appear, by private treaty arrangements. But, as should be obvious from the use of the term "private", it was almost impossible to determine from the record how these villages came into existence. In some few cases, the individual owners of the holdings can be recovered, and the location of the holdings and rough dates of acquisition were recorded, but in general no records exist that reveal either the sellers of the land or the price of the individual holdings. However, speculation in a few directions is possible. In the first place, that complex relationship which had developed between the employers (the planters) and their labourers, especially if those labourers had been formerly enslaved on the employers' plantations, still survived. It can be suggested that out of that relationship emerged actions which might be seen as benevolence, reward, charity, guilt or even consideration for the welfare of illegitimate children. It is possible therefore that such relationships created the framework for a species of negotiation between planter/owner and labourer which did result in the detachment of a plantation's marginal land. Secondly, as has already been suggested, the release of small portions of plantation land was the individual planter's response to the problems that plagued the sugar industry, particularly in the last quarter of the century. In other words, planters did profit from the strong demand for land which was being expressed in the high prices for small lots of land that they dispensed whenever they made some land available. It is true that some blacks failed to keep up payments on the instalment plans that the land speculators instituted, but such cases seemed to be few, and these were not unexpected in an era of low and declining wages and reduced employment opportunities.

Third and obviously, the demand by blacks for land, the basis of free village development, was strong and growing. This could be seen in the alacrity to purchase lots whenever the opportunity arose; and there was every reason to suppose that many blacks, if not most of them, took the initiative in those private treaty negotiations which resulted in the detachment of small portions of the plantation's acreage. Moreover, that demand could be seen in the activities of land speculators and in the generally high prices for whatever land that came on the market. It is worth noting that, while property values, expressed through the sale prices of whole plantations, was tumbling (and whole plantations could not attract buyers even at £26 per acre), the land that was sold in small lots could cost as much £160 per acre, but usually was sold at £70 to £90 per acre.[11]

The responses of both parties that were intimately involved in the presence and increase in the number of free villages admitted of no middle ground. For the blacks, the issue was Dickensian: they wanted more – more land at prices that were not "exorbitant". The opportunity to make their case was presented at sittings of the West India Royal Commission which in 1897 investigated the effects of bounty-fed beet sugar on the economy of the British Caribbean territories. Basically, the blacks' representatives or spokesmen made three points. First, "the people", as Archibald Dowridge put it, "were willing to buy land" because, according to Charles Alleyne, "the ambition of every Barbadian" was "to own a piece of land", but they were being hindered by the "exorbitant" prices being charged for smallholdings. Second, they claimed that there was "a settled policy", executed by the Court of Chancery, not to subdivide the indebted plantations that it controlled and therefore it was acting "to prevent a peasant proprietary from rising in our midst". Third, they proposed in consequence that the Court of Chancery should be abolished because it was "rotten to the core", that plantations in the Court of Chancery should be subdivided in lots not exceeding five and ten acres, that those lots should be sold at public auction, and that all the formalities for the land transfer should be made simple and inexpensive. In effect, then, they were proposing a land settlement scheme; for them, the potential inherent in village development, like central factories, would be "the salvation" of the colony.[12]

However, the policymakers, who were the leading planters and top officials, were dismissive of what had occurred and of what was possible. Presumably, they were unimpressed because the presence of free villages made no appreciable difference to the quantity and price of labour in the sugar industry, as they could depend on metropolitan support for their conviction that the blacks were forever destined to be plantation labourers, and because, for them, the problems that faced the economy (and the country) were those of survival from the beet sugar crisis. Therefore, the plantocrat, A.J. Pile, declared that "there is no excess of demand for small holdings over the supply" because "one or two small plantations have been recently sold out in small holdings". Pile did not name the plantations which had been recently subdivided, but the extent of his lack of concern could be deduced because he clearly expected that the subdivision of the 161 acres of the plantations, Greenwich and Newbury, could satisfy what he saw as modest needs. For Governor Hay, sugar yields "would rapidly decline" if the island fell into the hands of small cultivators because "the land would suffer from want of proper cultivation"; and this was repetition of the eternal mantra. Finally, Chief Justice Conrad Reeves issued what he intended to be a dire warning. If plantations were subdivided because sugar could not be produced at "moderately remunerative" levels, then "the present race of proprietors must go, and with them, the existing social and political status of the colony".[13] Of course, it must be admitted that these dire predictions were being made to bolster the plea for relief by the British government, but these opinions did represent the elite's longstanding evaluation of villages and villagers. In other words, that opposition, in dismissing any need for a land settlement scheme, was desperately making a case for its own salvation.

All this meant that there was no official endorsement of plantation subdivision, and therefore no official support for free village development, even during the period of extended crisis in the plantation sector. Land was theoretically available for purchase because indebted plantations remained unsold, but as the blacks' representatives had pointed out, that land could only be sold in plantation blocks because there was "a settled policy" to keep that land out of the hands of smallholders.

However, while it must be conceded that blacks' complaints to the West India Royal Commission were not completely unacknowledged, it was plain that no relief was immediately in sight. The Royal Commission, no doubt in response to both the representations of the labourers' spokesmen and to the evidence of the effects of economic depression, did at one level seem to favour support for the relief measures being urged. It said that, in the circumstances, "sugar land" could be subdivided, thereby providing some means of support for the labourers through "the growing of ground provisions or other crops". But, at the same time, the Commission dodged the central issues by not making a clear recommendation on these issues. It declared that the Barbados government "may facilitate" plantation subdivision, but it added a key rider: the Court of Chancery "must of course be guided by the interests of the persons whom it represents"![14] So, the central issue was left for determination by those who had "interests" to protect; after all, the Court of Chancery existed to protect the local indebted owners of plantation from immediate forfeiture of their plantations to British creditors.

Intensification of Free Village Settlement

Full note must be taken, however, of the extent to which intensification of settlement in many of the villages, old and new, buttressed the case for the appropriation of more plantation land. Examples abounded, particularly in the parishes of St George and St Michael. Take for example the parish of St George and observe what was happening in its two largest villages. At Airy Hill, Peter Chapman, in establishing his "farming lots" between 1853 and 1866, had laid out and disposed of the forty-seven acres in at least twenty-nine lots that each contained one to three acres. However, in 1893, the village, no larger than its original forty-seven acres, contained seventy-two holdings. As could be expected, only fourteen of those holdings were an acre or more in extent, while as many as thirty-eight were a quarter an acre or less in size. Much the same was evident at Workmans. In 1856, Peter Chapman had laid out at least fifty-six lots that were one and two acres in extent on the 102-acre property, and those lots had been sold to members of the new working class. But, in 1893, the owners of holdings in the village numbered 136, which meant that, for the most part, each landowner possessed less than one acre. Consequently, most of the farming lots in the village, like those at Airy Hill, had been reduced to large house-spots.[15]

St Michael: Parish Example of Free Village Growth

The parish of St Michael probably presented the best example of both the increase in the number of villages and the intensification of village settlement. This case can be presented because, unlike the other parishes, its 1852 parish rate book permitted a rough comparison with the data that can be derived from the records for 1900–1901. First, that comparison confirmed the significant increase in the number of the villages. For example, the settlement areas at Government Hill, Hothersal Turning and My Lord's Hill might not in 1852 have met the minimum qualification to be counted as villages, but by 1900, Hothersal Turning, the smallest of these settlement areas, contained at least eighteen holdings. Second, there was abundant evidence that the growth in the number of villages was not matched by a commensurate increase in the acreage in those villages. For example, Bibby's Lane (or "Near Lears") was recorded in 1852 as consisting of ten holdings spread over twelve acres. But, in 1900, the twenty-three holdings in that village were recorded as occupying a mere eight acres. Similarly, there seemed to be no significant expansion of acreage in the extended Black Rock District. In 1852, this large district or extended village covered about 110 acres and contained about eighty-five holdings that were five acres and under in size. However, in 1900, this area, containing the settlements of Chapel Hill, Danesbury, Deacons Rd., Eagle Hall, Free Hill, the Ramparts, Spring Garden and Wavell Avenue, contained more than 120 holdings which were apparently spread over an equal acreage. Therefore, it is possible to see a double process at work: new villages were being formed while settlement in several of the existing villages was intensifying.

This intensification was particularly evident at Bibby's Lane. In that village in 1900, only one holding was recorded as an acre in size, but eleven of the other holdings were a quarter of an acre in extent. This suggested that the land shortage for the emancipated was being expressed through the subdivision of smallholdings. This process, already noted in the parish of St George, seemed to indicate that the emancipated and their descendants were clearly practising their own versions of bequests of land through in-family subdivision of small property. This suggested that, in an age of property qualification for the exercise of the franchise, several of the original villagers were placing a greater premium on family welfare than on retaining intact the property which would have qualified them for the exercise of the franchise. This did mean that this subdivision of their holdings did delay a realization of that political potential which had been briefly displayed in 1848/49 at Rock Hall in the parish of St Thomas.

The "Lands"

The workings of that double process can also be seen in the spread of *lands*. This was the name that was given to the non-plantation tenantries that were born, mainly in the parish of St Michael, as a consequence of rural to urban migration. Essentially, those communities, carrying the names of the owners/landlords and landladies, were the settlement areas, close to Bridgetown, that were established by members of the rural population who had been displaced by planters' policies of retrenchment and reduced wages. The important point to notice was that the settlement areas for these internal migrants were located in already established villages, in Deacons Road and Eagle Hall, Green Hill and Codrington Hill, My Lords Hill and Government Hill, Collymore Rock and Brittons Hill. Therefore, it could be said that this influx of residents did intensify the development of established villages because landlords/landladies were emerging who could charge the new residents with the payment of rent for house and ground on premises that the owners most likely occupied.

The pertinent question, however, was whether this intensification of village settlement could be said to have created new free villages. There can be little doubt that, in the age of universal adult suffrage, those settlement areas, because of their compactness, were recognized as separate polling divisions and therefore could be treated as villages in their own right. But there is abundant doubt about whether that fact of separate existence was clearly recognized before the 1950s. After all, while the number of these internal migrants, and possibly their similar points of origin, probably spoke to separateness, this population can be seen as transients, especially during the first years of their new residence. Some of them would emigrate and others might move on to more permanent locations. Therefore, the test of full community existence for the new residents was the extent to which they were acknowledged as residents or became long-term residents. But there was another point. Though these new residents did not have to perform labour services for their landlords/landladies as a condition of continuing residence, obviously they were not in full control of the house and/or ground that they occupied. They could be evicted. This, then, is another way of saying that the new residents of these villages may have been part of a process of creating at least mini-villages if long presence in these new locations eventually led to pressure for purchase and actual purchase of the holdings that they occupied. It was only then that Burke's Land, Crawford Land, Dodson Land, Forde's Land and the roughly forty other eponymously named Lands, Gaps and Roads, might be designated as villages.

Thus, by the end of the nineteenth century, it could be said that free villages had spread across the island. That spread appeared to be uneven, with the villages being largely concentrated in the southern parishes. But that may have been an illusion because documentary records have not survived for six of the parishes. At any rate, however, the major features of the development were plain for disinterested observers to see. The number of free villages was large and increasing, but most of the villagers could only be distinguished from the agricultural labourers by location of residence. The explanation for this situation was that holdings in the villages were so small that most of the residents had to find sources of livelihood on the plantations that had been their places of residence. Most of these villagers could be barely classed as part-time farmers; they were artisans and mainly plantation labourers who did not reside in plantation tenantries. Therefore, in Barbados, there was a relatively slow movement in the direction of that social change, the tendency "to create grades in the social body",[16] that could be observed in most of the other British Caribbean countries.[17] However, this development, though slow, could hardly justify the comment that the *Pall Mall Gazette* made in 1881, when it reviewed the progress of "Negro Peasant Proprietors", particularly in Jamaica. It said then that "save only in hopelessly bestridden Barbadoes", the West Indian Negroes in a short lifetime had passed "from the condition of absolute slavery to that of peasant proprietorship".

FIVE
Remittances and Plantation Subdivision

Free village development in this third phase, 1905–45, was markedly different from all previous free village development in at least one particular. Most of the new free villages replaced, either wholly or in part, several plantations and small properties, with the consequence that free villages became the residential spaces of a majority of the rural population. That point can be put in full perspective by noting that, while this third phase saw the creation of fifty less villages than in the previous phase, it witnessed the appropriation of more than twice as many acres of land as could be found in the 233 villages of the previous phase.

Table 5.1: Villages: Number and Estimates of Acreage and Number of Holdings, 1905–45

Parish	No. of Villages	Est. Holdings	Est. Acreage
St Lucy	35	1,034	744
Christ Church	26	1,045	830
St James	20	1,390	668
St John	19	469	307
St Michael	16	1,968	1,058
St George	14	892	653
St Peter	13	602	341
St Philip	13	530	503
St Thomas	10	496	379
St Joseph	9	217	150
St Andrew	8	441	387
Totals	**183**	**9,084**	**6,020**

Sources: *Halcrow and Cave, Parish Rate Books, deeds in the BDA*

Map 5.1: Free Villages by 1945

Equally significant, the establishment of more than nine thousand holdings on more than six thousand acres meant that more than half of the former residents of the plantation tenantries had decamped from their tied residences on the plantations. But one of the basic features of village development remained unchanged because the small size of most of the holdings did not permit the emergence of a significant small farming sector. This meant that the majority of the villagers must have remained still tied to the plantation, not in terms of residence, but in terms of employment opportunities. Both situations must be explained.

The basic explanation for what, in the circumstances, was a large appropriation of land, can be found in the interaction of three factors. These were some prospects for the availability of land for smallhold settlement; ready cash by way of remittances in the hands of many blacks; and a facilitating agency in the presence of land speculators. Of all these, there is little doubt that the remittances played a cardinal role, but the role was only possible because it brought into play the other factors. It might also be noticed that those factors represented an important variation from what Sidney Mintz had identified as the "essential" conditions that had to be met before the "new freedmen" could become independent farmers.[1] That variation was the emphasis on the role of an agency for land transfer, and that agency, land speculation, must be highlighted because, in a small colony like Barbados, land for transfer to the "new freedmen" had been rendered difficult both by government policy and by the expressed opinions of the elite.

Prospects of access to additional land by the "new freedmen" existed at least in theory. The prolonged depression in the sugar industry, lasting from the 1880s until the outbreak of the First World War, had been mainly caused by ruinous competition with bounty-fed beet sugar. It had negatively affected sugar prices, the colony's place in a traditional market and property values. This had meant difficulties for many Barbadian planters who, with rising debt, could barely hold on to the possession of their plantations. Most of those who were located on the fertile soils of the parishes of St George, St Thomas and St John did manage to limp along, but most of the others were accumulating debt that they had no immediate prospects of liquidating. Therefore, the plantation sector was in a crisis that was barely eased by recourse to the Court of Chancery, by the operation of the Agricultural Aids Act, and later on, by the abolition of bounties on beet sugar.[2]

The local manifestation of that crisis on the plantation land could be seen in the statistics presented in 1897 to the West India Royal Commission. More than one-third (159) of the sugar plantations had been sold (as plantations) by the Court of Chancery between 1888 and 1896 at depreciated prices; the owners of 158 plantations relied on loans through the Agricultural Aids Act to remain in operation; and the Court of Chancery could find no purchasers for twenty plantations that it had advertised for sale. Moreover, 158 plantations were sold by the Court of Chancery between 1900 and 1919. But the point must be repeated: plantations were available for sale, but as plantations. Very little of that land that came to the restricted market reached the landless, the potential villagers.

Remittances, mainly from Panama and the United States, indirectly impacted this situation. Earlier supplies of remittance money, as George Roberts has shown,[3] had made an impact, almost certainly in land purchase, but that impact could not compare with the effect of the "stream of money" that now poured into Barbados. George McLellan painted the picture:

> Panama Money is no disguised blessing in the island, and one sees evidence of its sensible application all over the colony. On yonder hillside, little board and shingle houses, still unpainted, have sprung into existence, each being a home procured by some faithful toiler, whose remittances to wife, mother or sister, had arrived regularly. Those at home had pinched and thumbed the money so that there was a surplus from the cost of living to buy lumber for the erection of a cottage when the breadwinner at the isthmus returned home to ply hammer and saw in carrying out his darling wish.
>
> The little house erected, off he goes to Panama again, with an itching ambition to also become the owner of the land on which he has built his house ..."Panama Money" has worked miracles at Barbados and made paths smooth, which would otherwise have been hard and thorny.[4]

The size of this "stream" of remittances can only be estimated. Hard data on postal and money orders for the period 1901–20 are available, but the amount of other transfers, either by person or in the mail, can only be surmised. Therefore, George Roberts's estimates of nearly two million pounds sterling (or about one hundred million pounds in today's currency), might be on the conservative side.[5] But what was especially significant was the impact those remittances would have made on a depressed economy. Subsidies of normal living expenses would have featured at a time of retrenchment; houses would have been built and/or repaired; shops would have been opened; opportunities for secondary education would have been secured; and membership of friendly societies would have been boosted.[6]

The most significant impact, however, would almost certainly have been the boost that those remittances gave to the realization of that "itching ambition" to own a piece of the rock. Of course, it must be admitted that the possession of regular supplies of cash by some of the freedmen and freed women did not automatically translate into landownership; the imposing and public opposition to small-scale landownership still prevailed. Indeed, it was not until February 1911, when some plantation subdivision had already taken place, that the "peasantry" received any sort of public endorsement of their evident desire to own land. It was then that the lead writer of the *Advocate* newspaper responded to what he called "a preposterous proposal" from the *Agricultural Reporter* by giving limited support to what was plainly evident. He wrote that while "we would not care to see Barbados altogether converted into a peasant proprietary community", he saw no danger in a peasant proprietary coexisting with a "preponderance" of plantation ownership. The reason: "the occasional cutting up of an estate affords a safety valve to the thrifty peasantry".[7] Perhaps, he was just being realistic, but his comments carried significance because this was the first time that this social group had received any public endorsement.

However, the critical point was that several individuals, some of them highly placed, had immediately seen the profit-making potential that lay in the investment of remittances in smallhold land purchase. They had rushed in to divert into their own pockets the stream of remittances or the main tributaries of that stream. Therefore, one might say that the script which Joseph Bayley had drafted at Rock Hall in 1840, and which Peter Chapman had embellished, was now being acted out by a similar and larger cast some sixty-five or seventy years later.

More land speculators, products of the existing economic circumstances, therefore dominated the action. They had quickly recognized that remittances presented a means for both the struggling planters and the active entrepreneurs to gain access to significant supplies of cash in what seemed to be a long-running depression. Therefore, some planters or their agents either subdivided struggling plantations in whole or in part, and entrepreneurs found the cash to buy plantations out of the Court of Chancery (or from struggling planters) so that those plantations could be subdivided. Consequently, the scale of those transactions leads to the conclusion that land speculation was probably the only growth sector in the economy, at least up to the 1930s. Equally important, the number of plantations and small properties that were subdivided made the case for concluding that land speculators, of one sort or other, were the main agency of land transfer in this period.

These men, as before, were either of the one-off or of the professional variety. Into that first group could be placed individuals like C. Miller Austin at Vaughans in the parish of St Joseph, Samuel Browne who subdivided Kirtons in the parish of St Philip, George Evelyn who did similar duty at Mount Clapham in the parish of Christ Church, and Robert Haynes who presided over subdivision at Venture in the parish of St John. Into the second group, the professional or semi-professional land speculators, could be placed at least four individuals, James Challenor Lynch, Thomas Nathaniel McConney, Eustace Graham Pilgrim and Athelstan Watson. The extensive activities of this group of professional men certainly deserve more attention.[8]

The first of these men, in point of timing of activity, was Dr Eustace Graham Pilgrim (1863–1926). He had spent most of his working life in Argentina where he had been a rancher and a successful obstetrician. But, even before he finally returned to Barbados in 1909, he had since 1905 been acquiring indebted plantations that were being sold through the Court of Chancery. By 1913, this hard-nosed entrepreneur owned twelve plantations, mainly situated along the west coast (in the parishes of St James, St Peter, St Lucy), that contained more than twenty-five hundred acres, and these made him the biggest individual landowner in the island. He therefore had significant political and social clout, which was perhaps demonstrated by his membership of the House of Assembly between 1911 and 1924.

The important point, however, was his activity as part-time land speculator. Between 1907 and 1913, he sold about one thousand acres of his land (the marginal land of his large plantations and all the land of his small plantations) to would-be villagers. He is supposed to have justified his actions in his reply to his brother who had upbraided him for selling off "good" sugar cane ground. "You can go on planting cane," he was reported as retorting, "but I am planting niggers!"[9]

The next two men presented social and professional contrasts. Thomas Nathaniel McConney (1858–1921) came from humble beginnings to become a successful land speculator who used his profits to transform his social status. Barely literate, he started his working life as a shopkeeper/butcher, moved into livestock speculating, and then became a land speculator who owned seven plantations at his death. Along the way, he had participated, wholly or partially, in the subdivision of another five or six plantations, most of which he had bought out of the Court of Chancery. Therefore, his participation in the transfer of about six hundred acres became noteworthy because of his own social origins.

James Challenor Lynch (1858–1937), a man of mixed ethnicity, was, by contrast, from birth a man of at least middle-class standing. He was a graduate of Cambridge University, had qualified as a barrister from one of the Inns of Court, and he had left a thriving law practice in Jamaica in 1888 to take over his father's highly successful commission agency, J.A. Lynch & Co. He was the man who took the lead in professionalizing the business of land speculation by organizing groups of like-minded men to secure loans to purchase plantations out of the Court of Chancery and to subdivide and then sell the subdivided plantations to land-hungry Barbadians. As a result, he was involved, to a greater or lesser degree, in the subdivision of ten plantations that were mainly located in the parish of St Michael.[10]

Athelstan Watson (c. 1880–1933), the last of this group, can be regarded as the prince of the land speculators. This Englishman, who described himself as a "planter" when he appeared before the 1929 Sugar Commission, lived in Barbados for fourteen years, from 1906 to 1914 and from 1924 until 1930. Though he told the Sugar Commission that his speculation in land started after 1924, there was clear evidence that he had been "selling out a number of estates" from about 1907. He and his brother had in 1907 purchased the Enterprise Plantation, located in the parish of Christ Church, which they immediately subdivided. Obviously, it was the profits that were garnered in disposing of 185 acres in 150 lots that had convinced him of the great potential in land speculation, for this became his major preoccupation on his return to Barbados in 1924. He then became involved, either as owner or as agent, in the subdivision of at least seven plantations that were principally located in the parish of Christ Church. Somewhat fittingly, he could therefore boast to the Sugar Commission that he had sold "about 1600 acres", and that "I have virtually sold all these lands, situated in Chancery Lane, Wilcox, and Pilgrim Place." Equally to the point, he recognized that remittances principally enabled the payment for his sales. "The people here have no money," he said, "but their friends and relatives send them the money. As a rule, the persons living on the land get the profits from it and the persons in America pay for it as they hope someday to return and live there. There is a number of new houses erected on those plots of land".

The *modus operandi* of the speculators, particularly the professionals, was simple and effective. They bought indebted plantations at rock bottom prices mainly out of the Court of Chancery, or they identified portions of their own land for subdivision, or they acted as agents for beleaguered planters. They surveyed the plantation land, divided it into usually one-acre lots, and then sold the lots to eager buyers. They had no need to advertise their impending sales. No doubt would-be purchasers in the vicinity of the subdivision may have had early notice that a plantation was "selling out", but all indications were that would-be purchasers rushed to the site whenever news of an impending subdivision was circulating. E. P. Boyce, Compiler of the 1911 Census, noticing both Eustace Pilgrim's land speculating activities and the role of remittances, reported:

> It is known that emigrants to Panama have not been forgetful of those left behind, and have remitted money, sufficient in many instances, to enable them to pay the deposits and obtain possession of small holdings. I have no doubt that the opportunity thus afforded of acquiring land on easy terms was sufficiently alluring to cause a large number of such persons to settle in St James.[11]

Examination of the facts, however, would suggest that "easy terms" could hardly be applied to this process of land transfer. First, the sale price of the lots remained exceedingly high, particularly when contrasted against the price of land in whole plantations (which could reach as low as £17 per acre) and with the regular wages of the plantation labourer (which were about seven and a half pence per day). Some examples tell the story. In 1907, McConney bought the lands of the Chimborazo plantation at £17 per acre, but he sold lots of that land at £36 per acre. In 1911, Joshua and Edmund Baeza paid less than £25 per acre for the lands of the Charnocks plantation, but they sold lots at £66 per acre. George Evelyn paid £22 per acre for the 343 acres at Mount Clapham plantation in 1912, but he then charged £75 per acre for lots of its arable land (though he did sell the rab land at £12. 10s per acre). In 1916, James Challenor Lynch controlled the sale of lands of the Whitehall plantation which had been appraised at £21 per acre. However, he and his partners sold the lands of the subdivided plantation at prices of £52 per acre in 1916 and at £100 per acre in 1917. Athelstan Watson thought that the price of arable land in whole plantations was too high at £40, but before 1929, on three of the plantations that he had subdivided, he sold lots at £75 to £100 per acre. By 1925, when all land prices seemed to have been rising, Louis Whitfield Clarke bought the Goodland plantation in the parish of St Michael at £75 per acre, and he seems to have sold the lots of the plantation land at prices which ranged between £85 per acre and £500 per acre. One can only presume that the high and continuing demand for small portions of land, coupled with official distaste for small-scale landowning, did ensure that, no matter how depressed general economic conditions were, the price of land to the landless would remain "exorbitant". Indeed, it is possible, as C.C. Skeete and Starkey observed in the 1930s, that the servicing of the purchase prices often rendered "uneconomic" the possession of the small lots.[12]

This probable "uneconomic" feature, the second part of the "easy terms", was created by what Athelstan Watson described as "the instalment principle". Briefly, that practice, institutionalized earlier by Peter Chapman, called for down payment of "a relatively small deposit", full repayment over a five-year period and interest charges during the period of repayment. This could be regarded as "easy" only in its first stage: the down payment permitted immediate occupancy of the lot. But the difficulty could and did arise with repayment. Regular receipt of remittances could go some distance in solving that problem, but there were always competing demands for that cash. Additionally, significant problems could arise during periods of reduced wages and retrenchment if the anticipated remittances did not arrive, or in some cases, if there was no remittance money available at all. This second probability is what Skeete clearly had in mind: the small landowner was "compelled to sacrifice the cultivation and manuring of the land and to keep himself otherwise as fully occupied as possible in order to increase his earnings".[13] Few cases of dispossession seemed to have taken place, but though Watson, by his own account, experienced few problems with the payment of instalments, he recognized that a continuing threat to the stability of the class of small landowners was the absence of a peasants' loan bank. Such a bank was not established until 1937.

In any event, the activities of the speculators, spurred by the blacks' evident desire to own land, created a modest redistribution of the landed resources. Information, mainly culled from the deeds and the parish rate books, suggested that by the 1930s as many as sixty-nine plantations and fifty-four small properties had been wholly subdivided, and that an additional forty-six plantations had been partially subdivided. This meant that nearly two hundred new free villages had been created, that older villages had been extended, and that about ten thousand acres had been appropriated by the freedmen.

That appropriation of land was island-wide, but the spread was somewhat uneven. It was most evident in Christ Church and St Michael; it was moderate in St Lucy, St George and St James; and it was still noticeable in all the other parishes except St Joseph, where it was not significant. But, overall, it meant that the observation made by Dr John Saint, the director of agriculture, which was repeated by T.O. Phillips to the 1930 Sugar Commission, still held true: the sale of a plantation in small lots was far more profitable than the sale of a plantation as a single piece of property.

However, before the parochial features of this development are examined in any detail, the public reaction to it should be noticed. That reaction, so far as it was forthcoming, seemed to be a mixture of formal opposition and watchful acceptance that almost amounted to indifference. Very predictably, it was the planters' organ, the *Agricultural Reporter* which, in February 1911, delivered the first broadside. It declared that "the destruction of sugar plantations" through subdivision was "manifestly a dangerous procedure" because such destruction represented "the withdrawal of a source of contribution to the agricultural fund" because peasant farmers did not produce sugar and molasses. Moreover, it claimed, the labourers on the subdivided plantations did not necessarily purchase the lots; these might go to "outsiders". As a result, its argument went, the resident labourers would be demoralized and "a fillip to praedial larceny" would be the result. Finally, it supported a correspondent's suggestion that legislation should be enacted to limit the size of lots in all subdivisions to ten to twenty acres, and it also called on the legislature to "put a check on the destructive operations of the land speculators who cut up valuable sugar plantations and sell out the land to satisfy their greed for money".[14]

Nothing as outspoken as this was written or publicly said for the next three or four decades. However, it can be deduced that opinion at the level of the *Agricultural Reporter's* subscribers had to be mixed for a variety of reasons. First, some of the highly placed men were involved in land speculation, and some individual planters were acting, as they had always done, by selling off small portions of their plantations. Second, the government did not ease its policy on either Court of Chancery sales of the land of indebted plantations or, when it was egged on by "do-gooders", on the necessity for maintaining adequate sanitation in the "lands" around Bridgetown. Third, there was probably a measure of agreement with the stance that that the *Advocate* had taken: instead of "a community of only large planters and labourers", there should be "room for a robust middle class".[15] In the final analysis, the reaction over the period perhaps bordered on the indifferent because village development, for those not blinded by ideological convictions, posed no threat to ample supplies of labour to the plantations. This can be confirmed mainly through examination of the size of holdings in the new villages (table 5.2).

The parishes, as before, can be grouped, this time by the number of new villages and, particularly, by the number of smallholdings that could be found in each parish. Three groups emerged: those four parishes that contained more than a thousand holdings; the three parishes that contained between five hundred and a thousand holdings; and the four parishes that accommodated less than five hundred holdings. Similarly, villages might be denominated as: large (more than one hundred holdings); medium-sized (more than fifty and less than one hundred holdings); and small (less than fifty holdings).

Table 5.2: Holdings in Third Phase Villages

	Villages	No. of Holdings	Acreage	Av. Size per Holding
St Michael	16	1,968	1,058	.54 of an acre
St James	20	1,390	668	.48 of an acre
Christ Church	26	1,045	830	.79 of an acre
St Lucy	35	1,034	744	.72 of an acre
St George	14	892	653	.73 of an acre
St Peter	13	602	341	.57 of an acre
St Philip	13	530	502	.95 of an acre
St Thomas	10	496	379	.76 of an acre
St John	19	469	307	.65 of an acre
St Andrew	8	441	387	.88 of an acre
St Joseph	9	217	150	.69 of an acre
Totals	**183**	**9,084**	**6,019**	**.65** of an acre

Sources: Halcrow and Cave, Parish Rate Books, and deeds in BDA

The four parishes in the first group, St Michael, St James, Christ Church and St Lucy, shared some environmental features which partly accounted for the relative density of free villages and especially for the number of smallholdings. For the most part, these areas or districts, as the geographers have pointed out, contained long coastal strips, possessed much shallow black soils, and experienced long periods of drought. Therefore, as Starkey said of the Bridgetown district, it was "not surprising" that, in times of depression, "many" of the plantations were subdivided;[16] and it became clear that plantation subdivision was more pronounced in those parishes than in the others. But, at the same time, some local factors one might suggest that other factors were in play in each of the parishes.

St Michael was the site of the capital town and of the main port, which had made it a magnet for internal migrants, particularly since the 1860s.[17] Pressure on living space, especially when coupled with remittances, ensured that both land speculators and struggling planters would maximize profit-taking opportunities as the internal migrants searched for employment and/or opportunities to emigrate. Therefore, the parish was a happy hunting ground for land speculators: at least fifteen plantations plus several small properties were subdivided during the phase. As a result, as many as nine large villages were formed; the parish was the site of three (Bush Hall, Haggatt Hall, Goodland) of the five largest villages in the entire island; and the parish possessed island's largest village (Bush Hall) in terms of holdings, and also the largest village (Haggatt Hall) in terms of acreage. But what was also striking was that only two of the villages, Haggatt Hall and the small village of Lazaretto, possessed holdings that equalled or exceeded one acre. In other words, most of the holdings in fourteen of the sixteen new villages were little more than house-spots.

The parish of St James, because of its previous history, seemed to experience a surprising climb to this top tier in the classification of number of holdings (and villages). Previously, that parish had contained no more 207 holdings in thirteen villages, but in this third phase, the number of holdings had jumped by nearly twelve hundred, while the number of villages had increased to thirty-three. The only factor that did not show similar increase was the acreage of the villages. Explanation of this strange performance demands an explanation that goes beyond the environmental one. Proximity at its southern end to Bridgetown no doubt enabled residents from the north of the island to employ the parish as a corridor to the capital town. But that was a minor consideration when attention is focused on the land speculation activity of Dr Eustace Pilgrim. At least seven villages (Lower Carlton, Mt. Standfast, Porters, Reids Bay/Weston, Sion Hill, Upper Carlton, Westmoreland) were formed as a result his partial subdivision of plantations that were mainly located along the coast of the parish. As a direct result, the parochial treasurer could claim in 1911 that there were 1,767 "peasant proprietors", a third of them being women whom, he had been told, "had recently come from other parishes".[18]

All those villages, with the exception of Westmoreland, were large villages, and Durants should be added to this group. The remainder of the villages, with the exception of Sea View, were in the small category. But, the final point to notice was that, by 1945, the average size of holding was less than half an acre, the lowest of all parishes.

The parish of Christ Church retained a leading position as the home of free villages. The parishes of St Michael and St James accommodated more holdings; and only in St Michael was there a larger portion of land that was appropriated by villagers. However, Christ Church parish stood out primarily for being home to numerous free villages. With twenty-six newly established villages – second only to the thirty-five reported in St Lucy parish – combined with the earlier settlements, Christ Church accounted for nearly 20 per cent of all the free villages that were formed. That steady rise in the creation of villages could be attributed to two factors. First, the parish continued to be a corridor to the urban centre that was used by internal migrants. Second, and of greater importance in the circumstances, the parish, almost to the same extent as the parish of St Michael, was an active site for land speculation. This parish was Athelstan Watson's base: his subdivision of plantations created free villages at Enterprise, Pilgrim Place, Rockley and Wilcox; the Baeza brothers did the same at Charnocks; and a host of planters or their agents did cash in on the presence of remittances through plantation subdivision.

Those factors more or less account for the comparatively large number of holdings. For fairly obvious reasons, these holdings were far less than St Michael's, and St James was the only other parish that contained a larger number. However, it must be noticed that Christ Church contained two large villages (Charnocks and Parish Land) and that the remaining villages in the parish were equally divided between small- and medium-sized. But the really significant point was that while the average size of holdings in five villages (Chancery Lane, Charnocks, Edey's Village, Hopewell and Wilcox) exceeded one acre, the average size of the 1,045 holdings in the parish was a little more than three-quarters of an acre. Therefore, one might say that this parish, because of environmental reasons, corridor attributes and land speculators' activity, maintained a high concentration of villages. It might also be said that, because it was something of a corridor, it could not match St Michael in terms of number of holdings.

St Lucy, the fourth parish in the top tier, was the parish which contained the largest number of free villages (thirty-five) that were apparently created during this third phase. The number must be stated somewhat tentatively because the data on the actual formation of some villages cannot be retrieved. At any rate, the available information, mainly derived from Halcrow and Cave, indicated that, like the parish of St James, village formation sharply increased during this third phase. There was one large village (Checker Hall), three medium-sized villages in Hope Road and Bridge, Chance Hall, and Alexandria, and the remaining thirty-one villages could be counted as small. There may be two sub-explanations for this skewed distribution which was clearly a consequence of the subdivision of plantations and small properties. One was that only one large plantation, Checker Hall (320 acres), and one medium-sized plantation, Chance Hall (112 acres), were wholly subdivided by 1913. The second was that the parish, like Christ Church and St Philip, was home to several small properties which had survived the Sugar Revolution of the 1640s, and it was the subdivision of many of those properties that produced the small villages. Finally, it must be noticed that, in 1945, the average size of each holding was less than three-quarters of an acre.

The three parishes, St George, St Peter, St Philip, which constituted the middle tier, presented some elements of contrast. St George had been earlier among the leading group of parishes in free village creation. Now, in this phase, even though some fourteen new villages had been created, it had slightly slipped in position. St Peter, on the other hand, had not experienced significant free village development in the first phases, but this situation was altered during the third phase when thirteen new villages were created, and there had been a more than 600 per cent increase in the number of holdings. St Philip, like Christ Church, had earlier led the way in free village formation, but now, despite the fact that it was largest parish and possessed an abundance of marginal land, it had slipped in position.

Subdivision, and therefore the activity of land speculators, one-off and professional, was the stimulus to whatever free village development that occurred. In the parish of St George, the new villages, carrying the names of the plantations out of which they came, had been created out of the subdivision of one large plantation, Salters (294 acres), and of a number of medium-sized and smaller ones, including Ellerton, Greens, East Lynn, Prerogative and Superlative. The result was the creation of three large villages (Ellerton, Greens, Salters), five of medium size, and six that were small. In St Peter, the path was roughly similar. One large plantation (Ashton Hall, 213 acres) and a few smaller ones (Farm, The Whim, Battaleys, Sweet Home and Sweet Field) were the bases of the 602 holdings that could be found in 1945. Significantly, the average size of holding in both parishes did not even reach three-quarters of an acre. In the parish of St Philip, there was relatively slow growth in village formation: only thirteen new villages compared with forty-seven in the previous phase. The possible explanations embrace opposite tendencies: intensification of settlement in the earlier villages and an increasing amount of migration, both internal and external. In any case, the parish possessed eleven small villages and merely two large village clusters. Those two large villages must be identified because these were clearly the result of land speculators' activity: Kirtons owed its existence to Samuel Browne's subdivision; and James Challenor Lynch participated in the subdivision of Marchfield. But, perhaps, the most significant feature of village development in the parish was was the emergence of the small farming sector, which was reflected in the average size of the holdings. At nearly one acre, this was the largest average holding size on the island.

The other four parishes were marked by a relatively low incidence of village creation and of smallholdings. The parish of St John might be separated from the others in one regard, that is, in the establishment of villages. Nineteen villages, or about 60 per cent of all the free villages that were established in the parish during the three phases, were created during this phase. However, this scale of village creation was not reflected in either the total number of holdings or in the presence of large villages. Only Venture qualified as a large village; Sherbourne and Edge Cliff can be classified as medium-sized villages; and the remainder of the villages were small, ranging in the number of holdings from five to forty-four. At the same time, the total number of holdings in numerous villages was less than five hundred. The basic explanation for these developments was that St John, like St Thomas and St George, was a planter's parish, meaning that the fertility of much of the soil ensured that the plantation had a chance of survival even in a long-running depression. Therefore, little plantation land was subdivided: only a few plantations, medium-sized or small, like Venture, Sherbourne, Edge Cliff and Cliff Cottage, surrendered their land. That also meant that the average size of a smallholding was less than two-thirds of an acre.

The parish of St Thomas accommodated only ten new villages and less than five hundred holdings. This was not surprising because it could be classified as a planters' parish, containing much fertile soil, which meant that the plantation-based cane sugar industry had distinct prospects of survival even in the worst of times. As a corollary, free village development was modest because few plantations, large or small, were subdivided. In the event, two fairly large plantations (Hillaby and Welchman Hall) and a very small one (Arthur Seat) had been supplanted by two large and eight small villages. The average size of the 464 holdings was three-quarters of an acre.

The last two parishes in this group, St Andrew and St Joseph, shared some features. These parishes had relatively small populations, possessed some hilly country, and were the main home of the Scotland District, where land slippage was frequent; and those factors almost certainly explained the relatively slow growth of free villages. However, the statistics indicated that village development, judged by the presence of holdings, was steady in St Andrew, but it had stalled in St Joseph, most likely because of substantial out-migration. In any event, St Andrew did possess among its eight villages one large village (St Simon's), two of medium size (Cane Garden and Rock Hall), and five small ones. In St Joseph, among its nine villages, there was no large village and only one

(Airy Hill) that was medium-sized. The average size of holding in both parishes, though slightly higher in St Andrew, was about three-quarters of an acre.

Overall, then, village creation in this phase made a discernible dent in the plantation's apparent monopoly of the land. The transfer of about nine thousand or ten thousand acres, the result of actual sales by land speculators and of the extension of settlement in older villages, meant that the settlement pattern across the entire island had been altered. It is true that this alteration in settlement patterns could be seen most vividly in the parishes of St Michael, Christ Church and St James, but the entire picture of settlement bore little resemblance to that of 1840. At that point, the black Barbadians, apart from those few who had managed to reside in Bridgetown and in the towns of Speighstown, Oistins and Holetown, could be found, legally tied, on the four hundred or five hundred plantations and small properties. However, one hundred years later, at least 60 per cent of them had managed to escape the plantation tenantries by establishing residences that they controlled in the 485 free villages. Those villages, for the most part, were located on the marginal lands of formerly plantation land. Moreover, with no government assistance, the residents had tried, through kin networks, to actualize emancipation for most of their entire group.

That process, it must be stressed, involved two strands of development that were eventually compressed into one main tendency. One strand was a series of negotiations with planters which usually resulted in the detachment of small portions, a quarter acre or half an acre, of plantation land. This was a long-running process which was no doubt sensitive to particular relationships and to economic circumstances. The second strand was the activity of land speculators which often resulted in the subdivision of plantations and the sale of one- and even two-acre or farming lots to the freed men and women. Therefore, the potential existed in those farming lots for a small farming sector to emerge, but that potential could be realized only if the farming holdings remained intact. But, as could be seen in all such subdivisions, from Rock Hall (St Thomas) to Workmans (St George) to Checker Hall (St Lucy), a form of family subdivision over a generation ensured that many, if not most, farming lots were converted into large house-spots. This, then, was the tendency, to place the family welfare, and by extension the group's welfare, above narrow economic and political considerations.

The prevalence of this tendency can of course be seen in the average size of holdings. If exemption, for obvious reasons, can be granted to St Michael and possibly to St James, any examination will show that the average size of holding in 75–80 per cent of the cases seldom reached three-quarters of an acre, and that in only four parishes, St Philip, St Andrew, Christ Church and St Thomas was the average size of three-quarters of an acre achieved. Therefore, the socio-economic status of those new smallholders was not much altered: most of them could not be considered as small farmers. The change that village creation conferred was mainly psycho-social.

But, in the immediate circumstances, there was perhaps a more telling consequence. The vast majority of those who had deserted residence in the plantation tenantries had not found and could not find employment outside of the plantation. They might in some cases have changed their employers, but the real change was in the terms of employment. In short, villagers as "strangers" could earn higher wages because they did not have to compensate the planters for residential accommodation, but the plantation remained the main source of livelihood. From the planters' perspective, though this was never publicly admitted, village development and the reduction in the size of the tied labour force did not materially affect the plantations' labour supply. Put simply, most of the villagers, because they were not self-employed or alternatively employed, had no choice but to engage in plantation labour. Therefore, Barbadian free villages and villagers remained near to the plantation in more sense than one.

SIX
Role of Free Village and Villagers

Two issues need to be examined in order to bring into full perspective the role that the free villages and villagers played in the country's economic and socio-political life. One is the tally of the free villages, and the other is whether it can or should be determined if any special group among the emancipated people was mainly responsible for the establishment of the free villages, particularly during the first phase.

Tally of the Free Villages

The total number of free villages, spread over the three phases of development (table 6.1), was nearly five hundred.

Table 6.1: Tally of Villages

Parish	Free Villages	Est. No. of Holdings	Est. Acreage
Christ Church	91 (53)	2,126	1,701
St Philip	68 (38)	1,340	1,341
St Michael	61 (35)	2,656	1,594
St Lucy	59 (41)	1,309	954
St George	49 (44)	1,565	1,148
St James	33 (26)	1,597	813
St John	31 (25)	627	420
St Joseph	28 (24)	382	335
St Andrew	23 (15)	668	594
St Thomas	21 (20)	615	518
St Peter	21 (19)	738	420
Total	**485**	**13,623**	**9,838**

Sources: Halcrow and Cave, deeds in BDA

Those villages contained more than thirteen thousand holdings which occupied nearly ten thousand acres. Two points need to be made. First, the statistics in table 6.1 modify in a number of ways those that have been provided by Halcrow and Cave. Halcrow and Cave focused on *all* villages, but table 6.1 is an attempt to list only the free villages, partly because Halcrow and Cave seemed unaware of the earliest foundations. In addition, the list does not include any information on the 258 villages that Halcrow and Cave apparently found in their survey but for which they did not provide any information on either size or distribution in their Appendix V (a).[1] Presumably, those villages were either captured in their "Miscellaneous" and/or deemed unimportant. But the relevant point is that the surviving sources have revealed information on 485 free villages, and table 6.1 therefore presents Halcrow and Cave's tally of *all* villages in brackets. The second point relates to the estimated number and size of holdings in those free villages which are not listed by Halcrow and Cave. This has been addressed by including estimated numbers and size of holdings for those free villages. But it must be emphasized that those estimates are calculated at a minimum size in order to make allowance for mergers, changes of names, or the disappearance of particular villages.

Distribution of the Free Villages

The distribution of free villages across the island fell into two parts. Four parishes were home to more than fifty villages each (or nearly 60 per cent of all free villages), and the other seven parishes each accommodated between twenty-one and fifty villages. The explanation seemed partly to lie in land area: three of the four parishes with the highest concentration of villages were also the largest parishes. In addition, the high concentration in Christ Church, St Michael and probably in parts of St George seemed to be a product of both environmental conditions and proximity to the urban area. St Lucy is the parish that is left out of those calculations; perhaps the explanation for the surprisingly high number of villages in that parish relates to the subdivision of a number of small properties that had survived the Sugar Revolution. The only other point that might be repeated is that Christ Church's very pronounced primacy in free village development seemed clearly connected to environmental features and its corridor role.

Growth of Free Villages That Were Formed in the First Phases

Nearly the same pattern was repeated in the expansion of the free villages, that is, in the incidence of villages, formed before the third phase, that contained in excess of one hundred holdings. About thirty such villages could be counted, and most of those villages could be found in the same four or five parishes that accommodated the majority of free villages. St Michael led the way with seven such free villages, three of which, Black Rock, Haggatt Hall, and Bay Land (Bay Ville), contained more than two hundred holdings; and the other three villages of that size in respect of holdings could be found in St Andrew (Belleplaine and St Simons) and in St George (Workmans). Also of note, the parishes of St John and St Joseph did not reveal the existence of such impressive growth; but everywhere could be seen the evidence of the stimulus that remittances had made to both the formation and expansion of free villages.

Agencies of Land Transfer

Three agencies of land transfer can be identified. The first was bequests which were prominent in the formation of about 10 per cent of the villages, especially during the first two phases. The second was private treaty arrangements which were spread throughout all phases but were apparently most common in the first and second phases of free village development. The third was land speculation (or dealing in the sale of small portions of land) which could be found in all phases, but which dominated free village formation in the third phase. These two agencies, private treaty and land speculation, might be termed self-help, and these were responsible for most free village development.

Founders of Free Village by Special Groups

Various answers have been given to this issue. First, it must be noticed that, for the officials and the elite, this question seemed to be pointless. If a conclusion can be based on the very limited notice of this new social development in the written record, then the free villages were regarded as a necessary evil, and villagers were only worthy of attention when their behaviour seemed to be disruptive of existing social and political conditions. For example, the villagers at Rock Hall in the parish of St Thomas received extended newspaper coverage because they were seen as the main participants in the "long protracted controversy" that featured in the 1848 General Election.² Similarly, free villagers were accused in the 1870s of spreading insanitary conditions, and in 1895 the governor declared that they had incited the Potato Riot at Boscobel.³

Second, consideration must arise about whether the implied views of the historian-commentators, John Davy and W. G. Sewell, had any merit. For both of them, it would appear that the early free villages were mainly the creation of the "half castes", those who had inherited "the intellectual power of the white race", and that those villagers were the ones who seemed (to the authors) destined to wield political power.⁴

Thirdly, some consideration might be given to C.C. Skeete's general answer to the question. Apparently unaware of any nineteenth-century origins of the villages (and villagers), he posited the view that "the peasant or small landowners" included "persons falling within a relatively wide range of intelligence, education, occupation, financial position, ambition and industry", and that the presence of those characteristics produced "great variety" in the types of farms and farming systems.⁵

However, certain historical continuities seemed to favour Skeete's position. Clearly, as Hilary Beckles has observed, there were ranks among the enslaved during slavery, and it was reasonable to assume that those ranks no doubt influenced post-slavery social arrangements. The enslaved population could have been roughly divided into the "elite slaves" and the "rank and file". The "elite slaves", mainly Creole enslaved people, were head drivers, stock-keepers, watchmen, housekeepers, sugar technologists, artisans (carpenters, coopers, masons, mechanics), seamstresses and transport workers. At the bottom, the lowest rank, were "the rank and file", the field labourers. What was important was that this ranking was expressed mainly through perquisites: the "elite slaves" enjoyed better housing, sometimes they were entitled to enslaved servants of their own, and they received cash bonuses as well.⁶

At least three consequences flowed from those arrangements. First, according to Beckles, "many enslaved families came to see themselves as 'better' than others",[7] and no doubt they were committed at emancipation to maintaining that social distance from the rank and file. Second, the proximity to, or close relationship with masters and mistresses which the "elite slaves" possessed, no doubt gave them ample opportunities to engage in that species of negotiation which led to the hiving off small portions of plantation land after emancipation. Thirdly, their own privileged position usually equipped them with the means, or with an instalment of the purchase price, to acquire small portions of land at emancipation.

Unfortunately, full evidence about the status of the founders of the free villages in the first phase has not generally survived and therefore it cannot confirm Davy and Sewell's implied conclusions. However, the few snippets of information about the formation of the Rock Hall and Bridgefield villages (in the parish of St Thomas), two of the earliest free villages, provided some indications that might confirm Skeete's assertion. At least ten of the Mount Wilton labourers who participated in the foundation of the Rock Hall village in 1840 could be considered to be members of the "elite" group, but by 1850, civil registration data reveal that only five of twenty-four of the villagers were listed as "labourers", while all the others were fully employed as small farmers, artisans, drivers/superintendents, domestic servants seamstresses.[8] At Bridgefield, it would appear at first glance that William and Joseph Turpin, both men classified in the slave registers as "coloured" artisans at the Mount Wilton plantation, were migrating to the bought land at the Social Hall plantation in January 1841 in order to distance themselves from the "blacks" at Rock Hall who had founded that village three months earlier. However, a little scrutiny revealed that those *migrants* were joined by at least sixteen "black" individuals and that one of the leaders of that communal action, Callop Dayrell, was also classified as "black".[9]

Therefore, Skeete's depiction of the founders and residents of the new villages might be extended to take account of the action in the three phases of free village development. In that first phase, it can be expected that the former "elite slaves" would have been prominent because they most likely possessed the means and opportunities to achieve small landholding status. In the second phase, they and their descendants would have been increasingly joined by those of the lower rank who had needed time to accumulate the down payment on a small lot. In the third phase, prominence, at least in numbers, would have been achieved by the children and other heirs of those who had been "rank and file", particularly when the stream of remittances flowed into the country.

The Role of the Free Village and Its Residents

In a general sense, then, what seems to be crucial was the nature of the overall impact of this new development rather than the group identity of its founders. At the economic level, it was possible to observe at least three consequences. First, these new villages provided some opportunities for occupational differentiation. Sewell hinted at this development when he observed in 1859 that "the large increase of small landed proprietors, the number of coloured mechanics, merchants, clerks, and business men, in public and private establishments—all of whom make up the middle class—abundantly illustrate the industry of the African and his capacity for improvement".[10] While Sewell was clearly making a special case, it was undeniable that the villages, by providing residences outside of the plantations' tenantries for some of the formerly enslaved, could and did function as sites from which labour could be taken to the best market, did provide bases for the practice of some professions or alternative occupations, and even over time offered opportunities for the possible upgrading of employment options. A special word might be said about their involvement in shopkeeping. It would appear that in slavery and shortly after that the bulk of household goods may have been dispensed by "estate shops". However, with the increasing spread of residence (as well as the search for alternate and profitable employment) the village shop did make an appearance, and it did duty as both a business operation and a social centre.[11] In other words, the villages, like no other forms of economic and social development except education, carried the possibilities for the actualization of emancipation.

The second, potentially the deepest impact, was in agricultural output. That promise was early observed by Davy who had visited from 1845 until 1848. He described the "commonly large" crops that he saw on small properties: "there may be seen growing side by side, or intermixed, almost all the different vegetables which are in request in the island, – the sugar cane, yams, sweet potatoes, eddoes, cassava, ground nuts, and in some parts of the island, the cotton plant, ginger, arrow root and the aloe".[12] A century later, that variety was still in evidence, and some vegetables (carrot, tomato, bean, shallot, beet, cabbage, lettuce, okra) could be added.[13] But the promise of a regular and ample supply of food crops that seemed to be promised at the start of free village creation was never fully realized. This, at one level, was surprising because, by the third phase of free village development, more than half of the island's population lived in the villages, and the total area that was devoted to small farming had risen from about one thousand acres to nearly twelve thousand acres. The explanation seemed to lie in the nature of the farming system that was generally adopted and which might have given some indications of cultural rigidity.

This farming system, labelled by Skeete as "the predominating system",[14] featured an emphasis on sugar cane cultivation. Villagers, whether they were large or small landowners, full-time or part-time farmers, usually "halved" their land, with each half being devoted to sugar cane cultivation in alternate years on an annual basis. Therefore, while half of the land was being prepared for the next sugar cane crop, it served a dual purpose by providing ground provisions such as sweet potatoes, yams, Indian corn, cassava and eddoe. Additionally, "minor crops" like beans, okra, pigeon peas and sorrel were planted along the field edges. Moreover, to emphasize the primacy of sugar cane cultivation, the pen or farmyard manure was applied to the sugar cane space "just before the planting or in the early stages of growth, but always after 'provision' crops have been harvested"![15]

For a number of reasons, this was probably not the optimal use of a limited resource. First, the quality of the soil was in general inferior to that which carried plantation crops, and with the limited means to improve quantity of output by means of fertilizers, it was not surprising that the peasants' yield of sugar canes was way below that of the plantations. Statistics provided by Halcrow and Cave demonstrated that between 1940 and 1946 peasants produced an average of 15.6 tons of sugar cane per acre while the plantations produced 25.1 tons of sugar cane per acre.¹⁶ Second, the arrangements for the grinding of the canes to produce sugar and molasses took some time to be rationalized. In the beginning, as Davy observed, the villager paid the owner of the sugar factory with a portion of the product for the privilege of using his equipment, and then the villager assumed responsibility for the local marketing of the portion of the sugar that was returned to him.¹⁷ However, that process was somewhat rationalized over time, and the villager eventually sold his sugar canes to the factory owner who determined a price for the canes and would later pay "preference money" when the sugar was sold on the London market. Third, there were myriad problems that mainly stemmed from the villagers' junior role in the entire operation. These ranged from the informality surrounding factory owners' advances against the growing crop to factory owners' inconsistency in the pricing of sugar canes, to the arrangements for transporting the sugar canes to the factories, and even to the arrangements for the weighing of the sugar canes. All of these conspired to place the villager in an uncomfortably subordinate position to the planter/factory owner.¹⁸

The question therefore must arise: why did the villagers persist with a crop that generally seemed to involve small profit margins, occasional losses and informal manufacturing arrangements? The answer seemed to be that the villagers, left by the government to their own devices, were influenced by a mix of received wisdom and plantation practice. First, tradition held that the soil and climatic conditions favoured few export staples other than the sugar cane, and in any case, there was no general institution until the 1940s to spread information about agricultural knowledge and practice. Second, experience had taught that sugar cane was relatively easy to grow, especially three months after planting, and this was particularly important to those whose time was sometimes employed elsewhere. Thirdly, sugar cane cultivation promised the payment of a "lump" sum (sometimes two "lump" sums) which was equivalent to saving for expenditure on important items or projects. Fourthly, and perhaps most influential, was what Skeete referred to as "sugar cane sense".¹⁹ This was what all farmers had picked up after nearly three hundred years of the sugar cane enterprise: they had heard of "the crop", knew that it was the high point of the agricultural year and anticipated the making of a "crop" of their own. The only problem with this view and approach was that actual experience did not generally lead in other directions.

For the moment, however, the villagers' output of food and export crops might be tallied in order to demonstrate its weight in the economy. No figures detailing the size of the involvement of the villagers (peasants) in agricultural activity are available before 1940, but the statistics that were assembled by Halcrow and Cave for 1940 to 1946 painted an informative picture. More than 50 per cent of the peasants' land was in sugar cane cultivation and just over 40 per cent was being devoted to food crops. More important was the finding that villagers produced between 11.35 per cent and 14.35 per cent of the sugar canes that were delivered to the sugar factories.[20] But, equally important, it had become obvious by the 1940s that a measure of diversification could be detected in villagers' farming practices. For example, some attention was being devoted to the cultivation of cotton, and there was also specialized attention being accorded to the cultivation of some vegetables. All this, given a context of limited means and knowledge, must therefore be regarded as notable. Villagers broke little new ground, but their presence could not be ignored.

Villagers' spending power was the third reason why villages were impactful in an economic sense. Three points might be made. First, the extent to which the villages both widened and upgraded employment options would have increased, perhaps in a slow but certain way, the amount of cash that became available. If what Sewell observed can be verified, that is, that there had been a "very large" increase in the numbers of small proprietors and other members of a "middle class" by the 1850s[21], then it must follow that more money was in circulation. Employment options were widening; there was some emigration and hence some remittances; and more money was being expended at least in the building and furnishing of houses.

The second and more dramatic development was the impact of remittances, especially from Panama, on an island in prolonged depression. Remittances during the first phase, particularly from Trinidad and Guyana, would have made an impact during the first and second phases of village development, but that could not be compared with what transpired in the third phase. This point, which has been fully addressed by Bonham Richardson, demonstrated the continuing importance of remittances to the Barbados economy. What should be emphasized, as can be seen in Richardson's sample of the specific origins of the emigrants, was that those emigrants came from the villages as well as from the plantation tenantries all across the country, and that the remittances they sent or brought back would have gone some distance in re-floating a depressed economy. This was the clear result of the availability of cash for purchase of land, for the repair and the building of houses, for the launching of small businesses, for membership of friendly societies, for increased deposits in the Barbados Savings Bank, for some conspicuous consumption.[22] This meant that all sorts of business was given a lifeline, and that the stream of cash more than tempted members of the elite – planters, lawyers, and other professionals – to grab a piece of the action. All this can be tied to the villages. Villagers went to Panama; Panama Money created more free villages; and the free villages, old and new, became the conduits of remittances into the wider economy.

The third point can be said to be a combination of the earlier points. The third phase of free village development was obviously marked by remittances, but more than that, it was the period when the free villages became the characteristic place of residence for the majority of Barbadians. Therefore, even although the volume of remittances may have declined after 1920, the fact of the large increase in the numbers of individuals who were now residents in the in the free villages meant that upgrades in employment, extension of agricultural activities, and the increase of money in circulation, would follow. The greatly increased population of villagers was therefore the key factor.

The political impact, in comparison, was perhaps not as sustained until the 1920s and after. Before those years, there seemed to be more potential than actual deep political impact. The potential arose from the number who could meet the minimum income/property qualification for the exercise of the franchise. That qualification was freehold property worth £20 or annual income of the same magnitude, or payment of annual parochial rates of £5[23]; and in practice that was interpreted to mean that the owner of an acre of land plus a house had earned the franchise qualification. Therefore, at least one-fifth of the male villagers could qualify to cast a vote in the annual general elections. This was significant because the number of registered voters, at least in the 1870s, did not reach thirteen hundred, but the number of qualified voters was estimated to exceed twenty-four hundred.[24] Therefore, it follows that if more of the qualified voters had actually registered to become voters, then a discernible impact might have been observed.

Three points need to be made in this connection. First, the number of qualified voters could have been increased if many owners of farming lots had not subdivided their holdings in order to cater to the claims of kin. This practice was clearly seen at Rock Hall and Workmans, which suggested that family cohesion was perceived to be more important than political influence. Second, examination revealed that it was smaller landowners who generally did not register as voters. This was probably because they realized that, given the high property and income qualifications for candidates, they had little chance of selecting effective representatives. Thirdly, and probably of most consequence, until the 1920s, there was no island-wide organization or political party which in a sustained manner pressed the issue of the benefits of increased voter registration.

However, as to be expected, villagers were not inert in the political life of the country. In the 1870s, pockets of registered voters could be found in the free villages all across the country. Five or more voters could be found: at Cave Hill and Black Rock in the parish of St Michael; at Workmans, Airy Hill, and Cane Hill in the parish of St George; at Carrington's Village, Redmans Village, and at Rock Hall in the parish of St Thomas; at Holders Hill and Appleby in the parish of St James; at Cherry Grove in the parish of St John; at Dark Hole (St Sylvans) in the parish of St Joseph; at Boscobel in the parish of St Peter; and at Less Beholden in the parish of St Lucy.[25]

Moreover, that potential to affect political life was visible on occasion. It could most clearly be seen in what the *Times* complained of as a "perennial"[26] feature of the political scene. This was the controverted election, when a liberal-leaning man seemed to be defeating a member of the "conservative" group. This usually led to an allegation that the apparent result was caused by the casting of "bad" votes, and that therefore the House of Assembly should investigate in order to assure itself and the country that the voters concerned met the franchise qualifications. Such controverted elections were a constant in the 1860s: in St Joseph in 1861 and 1868; in Christ Church in 1863; in St Lucy in 1865 and 1866; in St James in 1866; and in St George in 1867.[27] What was important for our purposes was that most of the allegations centred on villagers' votes, and that the members of the House of Assembly, in a passion of self-interest, usually ruled that most of those voters had not met the threshold of property of £20 in rental value. Therefore, there is clear evidence that occasionally the villagers were frustrated in their uncoordinated attempts to derail the apple cart of the planter and merchants, and that, contrary to Hume Wrong's assertion, their actions did on occasion inject elements of "bitter political controversy" into the frame.[28]

Two examples might be cited. One, already noted, saw the eventually successful attempt in 1848–49 to unseat the sitting members in the parish of St Thomas, and that attempt caused "a long-protracted controversy". The second occurred in the parish of St Lucy in 1865. It was sparked when Horatio Nelson Springer, a middling planter of "liberal" views, and John Kellman, another planter, challenged the sitting members, Augustus Briggs, a planter magnate, and John Griffith, in the general election. The main issue in contention seemed to be the level of rates that had been levied by the parish vestry which Briggs controlled, and apparently that issue so stirred the electorate that an unprecedented number of the voters cast their votes in the election on 5 June 1865. That election drew a "crowd of people" which was described according to the political persuasions of the newspapers of the day. For the *Agricultural Reporter*, this was a crowd of "wretched Ragamuffins", but for the *Times*, the "humble freeholders" were the "numerous supporters" of Springer and Kellman. The first result of the election was, in the circumstances, a massive win for the challengers, but as to be expected, that result was overturned when the House of Assembly determined that the majority of the votes that had been cast for Springer and Kellman were "bad".[29]

However, no such firm judgement can be rendered about villagers' participation in riots, those violent forms of political action, during the various phases of village development. Those riots, judging by Henderson Carter's commentary and analysis, were frequent, pitting the "workers" against the planters (and authorities) in endemic resistance.[30] But, there was a simple reason for the absence of firm judgement about villagers' participation in that resistance: the villagers cannot just be lumped with those at the bottom of the social scale, and this complexity almost certainly affected how they responded to any issues of the day. Following Skeete, and without adding any complications that colour/shade might have introduced, there may have been have at least four different groups of villagers. These were the "larger landowners", owning eight to twelve acres, who did not depend on the land as a primary source of subsistence; the small farmers, owning three to six acres, many of whom were emigrants or the dependents of emigrants; the part-time farmers, owning between one and three acres; and finally, the owners of one acre and less, who were basically indistinguishable from the plantation labourers.[31]

The basic point was simple. Three of those groups, with some alternative means of support and with an asset, the land, valuable enough to protect, were unlikely to put the ownership of their land at any risk. The suggestion, therefore, is that they were at least neutral when violent action was contemplated or was occurring. Not so, however, for the final group; their status as property holders was little better than that of plantation labourers and consequently they were affected by whatever ailed their counterparts in the plantation tenantries. Moreover, because they constituted about 70–75 per cent of the male villagers, it could appear as though all villagers could be classified as the "workers".

In the event, there was only one reported occasion when the residents of the free villages were depicted as inciters of and participants in a riot. The occasion was the Potato Riot which occurred at the Boscobel plantation at the end of January 1895 when the potato fields were raided and protests were lodged at both a wage reduction and limited opportunities for employment. Governor Hay, in his report to the British colonial secretary, was clear about the cause of the riot: it had been incited by the people in the free villages in order to force the planters to start the crop.[32] But this is not to suggest that the villagers participated in a lone riot; it was merely confirmation that the bulk of villagers were always likely to behave like the resident plantation labourers whenever their basic means of subsistence were threatened. Therefore, it goes without saying that villagers, particularly those who were essentially plantation labourers, found it necessary to register violent protest at their deteriorating condition, through potato raids and cane fires, during the 1880s and 1890s.

The point can be taken further. The free village, because of the nature of the make-up of its population, was an obvious recruiting stop for all those liberal-inclined politicians, from Samuel Jackman Prescod and Samuel Francis Hewitt to Charles Duncan O'Neale, "Chrissie" Brathwaite and even to Grantley Herbert Adams, who, usually on an individual basis, tried to counter the vast political influence of the planter/merchant grouping; and the free village did give them limited prominence. But all that started to change from the late 1930s when island-wide political parties, the Progressive League (later the Barbados Labour Party) and Wynter Crawford's West Indian National Congress Party, rather than urban and suburban groupings, came fully into existence. The point is that the free village, with its substantial number of qualified voters, could make long-lasting impact when its numerical strength all across the island could be mobilized and when that strength could be expressed through a collection of candidates for the House of Assembly who had roughly the same basic programme.

That leaves for consideration the probable social impact of the free village. First of all, that impact might have been expressed through the building of community spirit. The full evidence of this must of course be left to the social anthropologists, but it is possible that the proof of its existence could be found in the spread of the village shops and in the foundation of Nonconformist churches and chapels. But the main impact was probably that the possession of even a smallholding made a huge difference in terms of self-worth or self-concept to each villager. That would seem to follow because the emancipated man or woman had seen and probably internalized the value of a possession of a "piece of the rock". Villagers would have recognized that possession of land usually meant wealth and influence; they would have understood that they could only begin to actualize their emancipation in the existing circumstances if, at the minimum, they possessed land which would enable them, if necessary, to take their labour to the best market; and that their own land, as a safety-net, could limit harassment by employers.

These points were all emphasized when Mary Chamberlain spoke to old villagers in the course of her research (in the parish of St Philip). She was told by an informant: "once you have your own spot, your house on your own land, you could work at Oughtersoon, you could work at Bushy Park, Harrow, Vineyard, anywhere...They couldn't fool around with me... they would always be more genuine with me, because whenever they start, I will tell them that I live in Gaskin, I don't live at Bushy Park...."[33]

It is therefore possible to suggest that free villages had some impact on labour relations. Of course, that impact may not have been general or deep because the planters, with a large pool of labour at their disposal, could, even with substantial emigration, still control employment possibilities. It is therefore more to the mind-set of the villager (a sense of independence) than to the actual operations of the employers that the point applies. It might also explain the increasing militancy (mainly through potato raids) that was displayed on fourteen plantations in eight or nine parishes in January to August 1895. Perhaps, then, it is possible to say that a smallholding of land in the villages carried "more than functional or economic significance".[34]

At the wider level, the free village was equally impactful. First, it increasingly altered aspects of demography, especially the patterns of residence and mobility. Before the 1840s, Barbados, outside of Bridgetown, was physically a collection of plantations and smaller properties where mobility for the enslaved population, the mass of the population, was restricted by "passes" or the necessity to travel by night. Emancipation had eased the processes of mobility, but the located labour system had tied the freed people, at least for working hours, to the plantation on which they had been enslaved. Now, however, with residence in the free village, the freed men and women had created new population centres which could cater to the search for, and the practice, of new employment options, and there was no compulsion to perform labour service for designated employers. It was true that in small Barbados these new population centres had to be located close to the plantations, but it must be noted that, especially after 1905, a substantial number of these villages had replaced the plantations in terms of land space, though the names of the plantations had been retained. Therefore, the physical layout of a few parishes, namely St

Michael, Christ Church and St James, had been significantly altered by the 1940s, but in all the parishes new settlement areas could be found on the marginal lands of plantations. In other words, the majority of the rural population lived in free villages by 1945.

This aspect of free village development therefore suggests what might be termed its contribution to social modernization. It cannot be over-emphasized that Barbados, before emancipation, was an incomplete society in modern terms because 80 per cent of its population was enslaved. Therefore, if Barbados by 1945 possessed at least the minimal characteristics of a developing *modern* society, it is reasonable to speculate about how that position became possible. It is suggested that, while education and sensible (or pragmatic) political leadership from the early 1940s might have been contributing agents, free village development was surely a part of that mix. This was so, not only because free villages represented the residences of most people. It was so because, particularly in the first two phases, it was the home of the intelligent, industrious and ambitious blacks, some of whom had managed to transform their own status in a professional sense. In that sense, the village became the incubator of developing social ranks in the community. The important point was that parents were most anxious to see that their children received the education that would ultimately transform their status and enable them to enjoy a life outside of the free village. This is not to say that the parents did not make their own contribution; after all, numerous cases could be found of clerks, teachers and politicians' henchmen who emerged directly from the free village. But the evidence, so far as it exists, would suggest that it was the children of the founders and long-term residents of the free villages who made a continuing impact. The suggestion therefore is that the residents of the free villages, often by one remove, provided Barbados with its professional class. Therefore, the free villages were critical to the evolution of a multi-layered society, which might be another way of saying that free villages were the stepping stones to surviving social complexities.

Notes

Chapter One

1. This aborted project was briefly reported on in Woodville Marshall, "Aspects of the Development of the Peasantry," 30–46; and in Thomas Matthews, "The Establishment of a Peasantry in Barbados, 1840-1920," in a paper presented at the 6th Annual Conference of Caribbean Historians, 85–104.
2. See Marshall, "Rock Hall, St Thomas: A Free Village in Barbados," 1–50.
3. See, in particular, William A. Green, *British Slave Emancipation*, 322.
4. R.T. Smith, *The Negro Family in British Guiana*, 13; S.W. Mintz, "Historical Sociology of the Jamaican Church-Founded Free Village System," 47, 65.
5. See Mintz, *Caribbean Transformations*, 230; and Mintz, "Slavery and the Rise of Peasantries," 242.
6. See instructions to Stipendiary Magistrates in Parliamentary Papers (PP) 1842, vol. xiii, appendix. Technically, police magistrates in Barbados were substituted for stipendiary magistrates, but they followed the same instructions.
7. That list can be found in the Barbados Department of Archives (BDA).
8. *Barbados: Water Supply Commission, 1885, with appendices*, 1884–85), 7–12, also deposited in BDA
9. See C.C. Skeete, *The Condition of Peasant Agriculture in Barbados*, 25–52.
10. See M. Halcrow and J.M. Cave, *Peasant Agriculture in Barbados*, 3–4, and appendix v(a).
11. See Colonial Office Papers (CO)31/67; and also, in BDA, *Return of Persons Liable to Militia Tax for the Year 1875*.
12. For example, the Parish Rate Book for St Michael for 1852 exists, but there is a gap until 1890–91; for St George, the lists commence at 1893; and for St Thomas, the surviving lists begin in 1935.
13. The most complete set of wills and deeds is held by the Barbados Department of Archives.
14. See Marshall, "Rock Hall, St Thomas: A Free Village in Barbados," 40–42.
15. The *Barbados Advocate* was responding to the vicious attacks on the land speculators who were being accused of "a dangerous procedure" of cutting up plantations in order to enrich themselves. See *Agricultural Reporter* 21, 23, 25 February 1911; and the response of the *Barbados Advocate* on 22 February 1911.
16. The late Frank Gibbons held this archive, and he must have passed it on to Louis Redman, who has since died. The present whereabouts of the archive is unknown.
17. Some of these Caribbean Studies are lodged in the Sidney Martin Library at the University of the West Indies, Cave Hill.
18. Knibb coined the term in November 1838. See J.H. Hinton, *Memoir of William Knibb, Missionary in Jamaica*, 304–5. Note, however, that J.M. Phillippo, another missionary, referred to these villages as "new villages". See J.M. Phillippo, *Jamaica: Its Past and Present State*, 220.

19. See Sidney Greenfield, *English Rustics in Black Skin*, 80–81 (footnote); also, George Gmelch and Sharon Bohn Gmelch, *The Parish behind God's Back*, 11–12.
20. Halcrow and Cave, *Peasant Agriculture in Barbados*, 3.

Chapter Two

1. David Lowenthal, "The Population of Barbados," 471. Such "line villages" can be found elsewhere in the Caribbean. See Raymond Smith, *The Negro Family in British Guiana*, 6.
2. See Bonham Richardson, "Livelihood in Rural Trinidad in 1900," *Annals of the Association of American Geographers* (offprint) 65, no. 2 (1975).
3. Hilary Beckles, *A History of Barbados: From Amerindian Settlement to Caribbean Single Market*, 62–78.
4. John Davy, *The West Indies Before and Since Slave Emancipation*, 148.
5. For a survey of soils and districts, see O.P. Starkey's *Economic Geography of Barbados*, 45–50 and K.C. Vernon and D.M. Caroll's *Soil and Land Use Surveys*. For the progress of the Sugar Revolution, see David Watts's *The West Indies: Patterns of Development, Culture and Environmental Change since 1492*, 176–231.
6. R.H. Schomburgk, *The History of Barbados*, 87.
7. Jill Sheppard, *The 'Redlegs' of Barbados*, 41–77; Hilary Beckles, *White Servitude and Black Slavery in Barbados, 1627–1715*, 141–76.
8. For example, see Ronald Hughes, "Sweet Bottom, St George, Barbados: An Early (1777) Non-White Freehold Village," 266–78.
9. Richard Dunn, *Sugar and Slaves*, 67. For an example of the worming out of small landowners, see John Scott's 1668 *The Description of Barbados* as transcribed by Peter Campbell in *Some Early Barbadian History*, 246–59.
10. See First Annual Report of the Leeward District Agricultural Society of 2 May 1847 as quoted by the *Liberal* newspaper on 5 June 1847.
11. This is the substance of the British colonial secretary's reservations and objections that were expressed in despatches in 1837 and 1838. See Colonial Office Papers (CO) 854/2 Glenelg to governors of West India Colonies, 6 Nov. 1837, 15 Sept. 1838; CO 261/15 Glenelg to MacGregor, 14 Aug. 1838; and in CO 29/35 Glenelg to MacGregor, 31 Aug. 1838.
12. Bentley Gibbs, "The Establishment of the Tenantry System," 23–45.
13. Henderson Carter, *Labour Pains: Resistance and Protest in Barbados, 1838–1904*, 29–30. See also Claude Levy, *Emancipation, Sugar, and Federalism: Barbados and the West Indies, 1833–1876*, 80–83; and Melanie Newton, *The Children of Africa in the Colonies: Free People of Colour in Barbados in the Age of Emancipation*, 227–47.
14. George Roberts, "Emigration from the Island of Barbados," 245–87; Carter, *Labour Pains*, 30.
15. Carter, *Labour Pains*, 23–28.
16. *The Anti-Slavery Reporter* 2, no. 7 (1841): 36; W.G. Sewell, *The Ordeal of Free Labour in The British West Indies*, 32.
17. Carter, *Labour Pains*, 84–96.
18. See CO28/188/48 Hincks to Labouchere 1 Sept. 1858. Data were collected from the following village sites: Vauxhall in the parish of Christ Church; Airy Hill, Campion Castle, Good Intent/Cane Hill, Workmans in the parish of St George; Cherry Grove in the parish of St John; Roberts and Cave Hill/Rock Dundo in the parish of St Michael; Bridgefield and Rock Hall in the parish of St Thomas.
19. Douglas Hall, *Free Jamaica, 1838–1865*, 20; Levy, *Barbados, Sugar, and Federalism*, 44, 79.
20. Parliamentary Papers (PP) 1842 (479) xiii, Appendix vi, Grey to Stanley, 19 April 1842, No. 12, enclosure no. 1.

Notes 105

21. PP 1849 xxxiv (1126), Colebrooke to Grey 27 April 1849, Governor's Annual Report for 1848; PP 1859, xxi Hincks to Lytton, 1Sept. 1858, no. 48, Governor' Annual Report for 1857.

Chapter Three

1. BDA, St Michael Rate Book, 1852.
2. This term was applied to those labourers who did not reside in the plantation's tenantry.
3. See William Green, *British Slave Emancipation*, 163–228.
4. See Alan Adamson, *Sugar Without Slaves*, 15–33.
5. The most relevant piece of literature is Sidney Greenfield's article "Land Tenure and Transmission in Rural Barbados," 165–76.
6. BDA, RB4/76/370, will of John Christopher Douglin, 13 Sept. 1852.
7. BDA, RB6/29/574, will of Patience Kennedy, 26 Oct. 1794.
8. BDA, RB4/66/225, will of Edward Brathwaite, 23 Apr. 1831.
9. BDA, RB4/75/485, will of Moses Brathwaite, 3 Nov. 1854; RB4/79/414, will of Sam Brathwaite, 3 Apr. 1868.
10. BDA, original will of William Johnson Bowen, 29 Apr. 1847; deeds: RB1/309/603, RB1/315/173.
11. BDA, original will of James Sealy, 1857.
12. BDA, RB4/77/585, will of William John Nurse, 6 Jun. 1853.
13. BDA, St Philip Rate Book, 1875.
14. BDA, original will of William Malloney Price, 9 May 1808.
15. BDA, RB1/292/73, will of Quaco Price, 29 Aug. 1823; RB1/305/166, deed of sale, 18 Oct. 1843.
16. BDA, deeds: RB1/240/93, RB1/310/315, 408, 310, 609, 694; original will of Sarah Price, 24 Oct. 1848.
17. BDA, original will of Robert Hudgwell Batson, 8 Jan. 1833; deeds: RB1/301/240, RB1/311/220, RB1/315/578, RB1/327/890; RB4/72/469, RB4/74/477 wills of Elizabeth James/Jane Batson and Alfred Batson.
18. BDA, RB4/71/196 will of Samuel Hall Lord, 8 July 1844; deeds: RB1/315/325, RB1/327/635.
19. BDA, original will of William Reece, 22 Apr. 1835.
20. BDA, RB1/317/707 deed of 13 Oct. 1853.
21. BDA, List of landowners, 1847.
22. BDA, deeds: RB1/305/87, 89, 95. A copy of the survey plan was donated by a land surveyor, the late Frank Gibbons, and it is deposited in the Barbados Department of Archives.
23. BDA, deeds: RB1/309/701, RB1/319/167, 898, RB1/316/201; RB1/309/258; RB1/318/160, 164, 166, 362, 364, RB1/312/570, 572.
24. See Woodville Marshall, "Rock Hall, St Thomas: A Free Village in Barbados," 1–50, which is the source of all the following information on the Rock Hall village.
25. For the *Barbadian*'s comments, see 22 Nov., 20, 27 Dec. 1848 and 7, 20 Jan. 1849; for the *Liberal*'s responses, see issues of 20 Dec. 1848, and 10, 17, 20 Jan. 1849.
26. BDA, will: RB4/80/588; deeds: RB1/309, 744; RB1/310/145, 279, 299, 314; RB1/311/233, 263; RB1/329/220; RB1/337/410.
27. BDA, deeds: RB1/308/442, 625, 702; RB1/309/713; RB1/310/1; RB1/318/631.
28. BDA, deeds: RB1/314/188, 414; RB1/315/299, 302, 352, 683, 686; RB1/319/66.
29. BDA, deeds: RB1/316/215, 232, 310, RB1/319/324, 677, RB1/320/187, RB1/322/799, 883, RB1/331/9.

30. The information on these villages is taken Woodville Marshall's article "'Designing' individual or 'celebrated solicitor'? Peter Chapman's activity and role as a land speculator after Emancipation," 6–31.
31. The anthropologist Sidney Greenfield, a century later, was still hearing stories about the pricing of the lots and about the re-possession of those lots. See his book, *English Rustics in Black Skin* and notice that "Enterprise Hall" is Workmans.
32. See, in particular, Hilary Beckles, *A History of Barbados*; Henderson Carter, *Labour Pains: Resistance and Protest in Barbados 1838-1904* and David Browne, *Race, Class, Politics and the Struggle for Empowerment in Barbados, 1914–1937*.

Chapter Four

1. BDA, *Report of Water Supply Commission, 1885*, 8.
2. Pertinent rate books exist for Christ Church, St George, St Joseph, St Michael and St Philip.
3. See Woodville Marshall, "Rock Hall, St Thomas: A Free Village in Barbados," 1–50.
4. For this period of near crisis and crisis, see R.W. Beachey, *The British West Indies Sugar Industry in the Late 19th Century*, 14–39; Celia Karch with Henderson Carter, *The Rise of the Phoenix: The Barbados Mutual* in *Caribbean Economy and Society, 1840–1990*, 72–85.
5. See G.W. Roberts, "Emigration from the Island of Barbados," 246–87. Note, in particular, his tables 4 and 6. See also *Royal Commission on the West Indies* [WIRC 1897] C. 8655 of 1897, responses to questions 345, 346, 437.
6. BDA, RB4/78/564, John Francis Gill's will of 5 Dec. 1863; RB4/79/711, Thomas Henry Straughan's will of 9 Jan. 1869.
7. BDA, RB4/80/202, George Christie's will of 21 Oct. 1869.
8. BDA, RB4/85/274, George Francis Holder's will of 2 Dec. 1883.
9. He seems to have been involved in the Barbados Land Co-Operative Co. Ltd, which was incorporated in 1888 and had pertinent objectives. These were the purchase of real estate and its re-sale to shareholders upon the Rent-Purchase System or otherwise.
10. *WIRC 1897: Minutes of Proceedings and Evidence*, responses to questions 212–17.
11. See *WIRC 1897*, document 223.
12. See *WIRC 1897*, responses to questions 875, 895, 913, 916, 929, 934 and memoranda 237–39, 241.
13. *WIRC 1897*, responses to questions 212–17, and memoranda 243, 246.
14. *WIRC 1897*, Report, 230.
15. See Marshall, "'Designing Individual' or 'Celebrated Solicitor'? Peter Chapman's Activity and Role as Land Speculator After Emancipation," 18–19; and see also St George Parish Rate Book, 1893.
16. John Davy, *The West Indies, Before and Since Slave Emancipation*, 153.
17. See W.A. Green, *British Slave Emancipation*, 295–326. It is noticeable what he writes about Barbados at page 321: "free villages did not arise".

Chapter Five

1. Sidney Mintz, *Caribbean Transformations*, 159.
2. See *WIRC 1897*, documents 206–16.
3. G.W. Roberts, "Emigration from the Island of Barbados," 282–84; Bonham Richardson, *Panama Money in Barbados, 1900–1920*, 155–56.
4. George McLellan, *Some Phases of Barbadian Life*, 73.
5. See B.C. Richardson, *Panama Money*, 155–66.

6. Aviston Downes, "Panama Money: General Effects," 121–44; Richardson, *Panama Money*, 170–232.
7. *Barbados Advocate*, 22 Feb. 1911.
8. What follows on these men is based on Woodville Marshall's article, "Remittances Villages in Barbados, c. 1905–c. 1935," 222–27.
9. The story was reported at a public lecture. For a less than flattering portrait of the man, see Clennell Wickham's *Pen and Ink Sketches and Other Essays of Barbadian Politicians*.
10. See Pat Stafford, "A Barbados Museum Founding Father: James Challenor Lynch and His Fascinating Family History," 62–73.
11. *Report on the 1911 Census*, 6.
12. See C.C. Skeete, *The Condition of Peasant Agriculture in Barbados*, 14–16; also, O.P. Starkey, *The Economic Geography of Barbados*, 45–46.
13. Skeete, *The Condition of Peasant Agriculture*, 15, 23.
14. *Agricultural Reporter*, 21 Feb., 23 Feb. and 25 Feb. all in 1911.
15. *Barbados Advocate*, 22 and 24 Feb. 1911.
16. Starkey, *The Economic Geography of* Barbados, 45. Most of what follows is based on the information that was published by M. Halcrow and J.M. Cave in *Peasant Agriculture in Barbados*.
17. See David Lowenthal, "The Population of Barbados," 471–80.
18. *Official Gazette*, 7 Dec. 1911.

Chapter Six

1. See M. Halcrow and J.M. Cave, *Peasant Agriculture in Barbados*, 3–4 and Appendix V (a).
2. Woodville Marshall, "Rock Hall, St Thomas: A Free Village in Barbados," 6.
3. See ibid., 37–38; Carter, *Labour Pains*, 166.
4. John Davy, *The West Indies, Before and Since Slave Emancipation*, 79–82, 148–54; W.G. Sewell, *The Ordeal of Free Labour in the British West Indies*, 68–73.
5. C.C. Skeete, *The Condition of Peasant Agriculture in Barbados*, 5 para. 2.
6. Hilary Beckles, *A History of Barbados*, 77.
7. Ibid.
8. *Register of Slaves*, 1821, 1834; Marshall, "Rock Hall," 38.
9. *Register of Slaves*, 1821.
10. W.G. Sewell, *The Ordeal of Free Labour in the British West Indies*, 43.
11. See Sidney Greenfield, *English Rustics in Black Skin*, 85.
12. Davy, *The West Indies, Before and Since Slave Emancipation*, 149.
13. Skeete, *The Condition of Peasant Agriculture*, 5–12; Halcrow and Cave, *Peasant Agriculture in Barbados*, 12–18, paras. 46–67.
14. Skeete, *The Condition of Peasant Agriculture*, 2–5.
15. Ibid., 4.
16. Halcrow and Cave, *Peasant Agriculture in Barbados*, 13, para. 50.
17. Davy, *The West Indies, Before and Since Slave Emancipation*, 150.
18. See *Report* of the Deane Commission, paras. 16–20; Halcrow and Cave, *Peasant Agriculture in Barbados*, paras 122–23.
19. Skeete, *The Condition of Peasant Agriculture*, 13.
20. Halcrow and Cave, *Peasant Agriculture in Barbados*, 13–14, para. 50.
21. Sewell, *The Ordeal of Free Labour*, 69.
22. See Richardson, *Panama Money*, 140–232.
23. *Laws of Barbados, 1645-1858*, No. 134, An Act to Amend the Representation of the People Act.

24. See Marshall, "List of Voters for Barbados 1873."
25. Marshall, "List of Voters for Barbados 1873," 194.
26. *Times*, 18 Aug. 1865.
27. Marshall, "List of Voters," 195.
28. Hume Wrong, *Government of the West Indies*, 86–88.
29. *Times*, 9 June, 18 July, 25 July, 4 August in 1865.
30. Carter, *Labour Pains*, 84–178.
31. See Skeete, *The Condition of Peasant Agriculture*, 5–8.
32. Carter, *Labour Pains*, 166.
33. Mary Chamberlain, "Renters and Farmers: The Barbadian Plantation Tenantry System, 1917–1937," 208.
34. Richardson, *Panama Money*, 193.

Appendix: Free Villages, Number, Approximate Size and Date of Formation

First Phase

Free Villages	Holdings	Acreage
Christ Church (18)		
Apple Grove (by 1847)	5	6 0 00
Birketts (1851)	5	5 0 00
Bournes (by 1847)	5	7 0 00
Bright Hill (1857)	5	25 0 00
Cane Vale (by 1847)	6	12 2 10
Cox Rd. (1853)	6	10 0 00
Dayrells Rd. (1847)	6	11 3 00
Friendly Cot (by 1847)	7	18 3 00
Gibbons Boggs (by 1847)	13	13 0 00
Harmony Hall (1848)	16	7 2 00
Lead Vale (by 1847)	6	24 0 00
Lodge Rd. (by 1847)	7	11 2 00
Maxwell Hill (1851–52)	5	2 3 00
Pilgrim Place (by 1847)[1]	17	17 0 00
Rose Hill/ Silver Hill (by 1847)	10	23 0 00
St Patrick's (1844–49)	5	6. 2 00
Vauxhall (1842–45)	11	5 3 28
Walronds (1850)	6	6 0 00

St Andrew (5)		
Cheltenham (1851–52)	8	9 2 00
Douglin Village (1852)	5	4 0 00
Licorish Village (1839)	5	22 0 00

1. The plantation was subdivided in the 1920s.

Free Villages	Holdings	Acreage
St. Simon's Village (by 1860)	10	10 0 00
Shorey Village (1841–42)	5	5 0 00

St George (7)		
Airy Hill (1853; 1866)	29	47 0 00
Campion Castle (1855)	9	10 0 00
Cane Hill/Good Intent (1848–55)	10	10 0 00
Dash Valley (1850–52)	5	8 0 00
St Jude's (c1847)	5	2 2 00
Waverley Cot (1851–54)	8	11 0 00
Workmans (1856)	56	102 0 00

St James (3)		
Endeavour Village/Orange Hill (1854)	10	10 0 00
Fitts Village (1849–52)	10	10 0 00
The Garden (by 1857)	10	10 0 00

St John (3)		
Cherry Grove (1853)	8	12 0 00
Massiah St. (1847–54)	5	2 2 00
Sarjeant St. (after 1839)	10	2 0 00

St Joseph (2)		
Free Hill/St Bernard's Village (by 1847)	10	5 0 00
Parris Hill (1845)	5	5 0 00

St Lucy (4)		
Free Hill (1845?)	5	2 2 00
Greenidges (1848)	6	15 3 00
Josey Hill (1854)	5	8 0 00
Northumberland (1858)	8	15 0 00

Free Villages	Holdings	Acreage
St Michael (13)		
Belle Gully (1852 Rate Book)	7	5 3 00
Bibby's Lane (ditto)	15	15 1 00
Black Rock (ditto)	85	110 0 00
Brittons Hill (ditto)	9	6 1 00
Cave Hill (ditto)	12	21 1 00
Codrington Hill (ditto)	18	15 0 00
Collymore Rock (ditto)	11	8 0 00
Haggatt Hall (ditto)	7	10 0 00
My Lords Hill (ditto)	8	11 0 00
Roberts Tenantry (ditto)	8	14 0 00
Rock Dundo (1847-48)	6	17 3 00
Two Mile Hill (1852 Rate book)	10	5 2 00
Whitehall (ditto)	5	5 2 00
St Peter (1)		
Gay's Land (1846–47)	6	10
St Philip (8)		
Bequest Village (1844–60)	20	50 0 00
Brereton (1846–47)	5	10 0 00
Duncans (by 1847)	9	20 0 00
Marley Vale (?1850)	10	18 1 00
The Nursery (1853–60)	10	15 0 00
Rock Hall (by 1847)	5	10 0 00
Supers (by 1860s)	10	10 0 00
Valley (by 1847)	9	18 0 00
St Thomas (5)		
Bridgefield (1841)	12	12 0 00
Chapman's Village (1862-67)	5	5 0 00
Redmans Village (1843–45)	7	10 0 00
Rock Hall (1840–44)	38	40 0 00
Whitehall (1847–49)	5	5 3 00

Second Phase

Free Villages	Holdings	Acreage
Christ Church (47)		
The Abbey (by 1905)	8	10 0 00
Adams Castle (ditto)	14	6 3 12
Bartletts (by 1875)	9	10 0 16
Breedys (by 1905)	7	7 2 00
Briar Hall (by 1875)	29	24 1 24
Brown's Bay (by 1905)	7	8 3 17
Burnetts (by 1875)	11	4 3 14
Nr Clarke's Court (by 1905)	35	34 0 23
Cocoanut Walk (ditto)	14	12 2 17
Nr Durants (ditto)	13	3 2 30
Nr Ealing Grove (ditto)	44	43 2 31
Nr Enterprise (ditto)	51	32 3 36
Evergreen Grove (ditto)	7	8 3 12
Nr Fair View (ditto)	17	19 2 11
Nr Goodland (ditto)	34	18 1 28
Green Gardens (ditto)	9	4 0 20
Nr Greenland (ditto)	10	9 3 14
Hastings (by 1875)	22	4 2 35
Nr Hill House (by 1905)	9	5 0 24
Nr Kingsland (by 1885)	33	21 2 13
Lemon Grove (1894)	7	5 2 00
Nr Lowthers (by 1905)	48	34 2 31
Nr Lyrias (ditto)	24	9 0 37
Nr Maynards (ditto)	23	13 3 22
Nr Montrose (ditto)	12	7 3 18
Nr Mt. Clapham (ditto)[2]	8	4 1 27
Nr Newton (ditto)	12	5 0 34
Nr Packers (by 1875)	10	4 2 22
Nr Pegwell (by 1905)	46	24 0 14
Nr Plum Grove (ditto)	9	4 0 39

2. The plantation was subdivided in 1912–18.

Appendix: Free Villages, Number, Approximate Size and Date of Formation

Free Villages	Holdings	Acreage
Rawlins/Rollins (by 1875)	44	34 2 16
Round Rock (by 1905)	16	10 0 08
Rucks (by 1875)	7	7 2 00
Nr Searles (by 1905)	9	5 1 16
Skeetes Hill (ditto)	10	8 1 27
Nr Social Hall (by 1875)	15	9 1 33
South View (by 1905)	10	9 3 34
Nr Staple Grove (ditto)	11	5 2 27
Nr St. David's (by 1875)	12	10 3 02
Thornbury Hill (ditto)	57	34 3 26
Walls (ditto)	22	13 3 00
Nr Warners (ditto)	85	60 2 34
Nr Welches (ditto)	11	5 3 18
Welcome Hall (by 1905)	9	14 2 24
Nr Woodbourne (ditto)	18	9 2 05
Nr Wotton (ditto)	14	7 0 11
Nr Yorkshire (by 1875)	8	3 0 00
St Andrew (10)		
Back River (by 1875)	10	5 0 00
Belleplaine (ditto)	30	25 0 00
Boscobel (ditto)	25	20 0 00
Dorants (by 1885)	25	20 0 00
Free Hill (ditto)	25	20 0 00
Hoyte's Village (by 1901)	10	5 0 00
Mt. All (by 1875)	25	20 0 00
Mt. Hillaby (by 1901)	10	5 0 00
Triopath (by 1885)	25	20 0 00
White Hill (by 1875)	9	16 1 00
St George (28)		
Baird's Village (by 1893)	17	6 1 00
Below Almshouse (by 1893)	11	11 1 31
Bourne Village/Cole Hole (by 1875)	19	12 1 04

Free Villages	Holdings	Acreage
Briggs Hill (by 1893)	24	9 2 27
Charles Rowe Village (by 1875)	5	5 0 01
First Step (ditto)	11	9 1 01
Flat Rock/Mess House (by 1893)	27	13 1 02
Free Hill (by 1900)	22	18 2 37
Holder's Village (1883)	6	1 2 20
Jericho/Nr. Jordans (by 1893)	10	3 2 39
Macaroni Town (ditto)	14	7 2 23
Mannings Land (by 1885)	9	7 3 00
Market Hill (by 1875)	30	21 1 30
Melverton (ditto)	21	13 3 24
Middleton (by 1893)	16	9 1 31
Under Mount Hill (ditto)	10	4 3 21
Munroe's Tenantry (by 1875)	18	13 1 26
Newbury (1893)	67	34 0 14
Old Post Office (by 1893)	27	15 0 15
Retreat/Nr Hilbury (ditto)	13	4 1 00
Retreat Wood (ditto)	25	8 0 15
Roaches (1876)	21	9 3 22
Rock Hall/Nr. St. Helens (by 1893)	14	4 0 20
Rock Hall/Nr. Walkers (ditto)	40	23 0 13
South District (by 1875)	21	12 3 04
Nr. St Helens (by 1885)	14	4 0 00
Taitt's Hill (by 1875)	14	8 3 04
Watts Tenantry (by 1885)	25	12 3 31
St James (10)		
Appleby Gardens (by 1875)	17	33 0 00
Baywoods (by 1906)	15	5 0 00
Curiosity (by 1875)	10	10 0 00
Greenwich (ditto)	30	15 0 00
Halls Village (ditto)	20	12 0 00
Holders Hill (ditto)	20	30 0 00
Nr. Hope (by 1918)	15	10 0 00

Appendix: Free Villages, Number, Approximate Size and Date of Formation

Free Villages	Holdings	Acreage
Nr. Oxnards (ditto)	15	15 0 00
Nr. Prospect (by 1875)	30	30 0 00
York Town (by 1918)	5	5 0 00
St John (9)		
Coach Hill (by 1885)	25	20 0 00
Edey's Village (by 1916)	5	5 0 00
Gall Hill (by 1885)	25	20 0 00
Glenburnie (by 1916)	5	5 0 00
Moore's Land (by 1875)	5	5 0 00
Spooner's (by 1885)	25	10 0 00
Stewarts Hill (by 1907)	10	10 0 00
Wilson Hill (by 1885)	25	10 0 00
Zores/Zoar (by 1900)	10	11 2 00
St Joseph (17)		
Bonwell (by 1916)	11	8 0 00
Bowling Alley (by 1875)	10	14 0 00
Braggs Hill (by 1905)	37	19 0 00
Branchbury (by 1885)	5	10 0 00
Cambridge (by 1875)	17	22 0 00
Cocoanut Grove (by 1905)	8	7 2 26
Coffee Gully (by 1885)	11	8 0 00
Farmers Village (by 1905)	7	3 0 00
Fruitful Hill (by 1905)	8	5 0 00
Hillswick (by 1905)	9	12 1 29
Melvin's Hill (by 1875)	7	9 3 00
Nowell Village (by 1905)	6	2 3 19
Orange Grove (ditto)	6	6 2 38
Shufflers Village (by 1905)	10	10 0 00
St Sylvan's (ditto)	20	25 0 00
Straughan's Village (1905)	9	3 2 00
Sugar Hill (by 1875)[3]	5	8 0 00

3. The plantation was wholly subdivided after 1907.

Free Villages	Holdings	Acreage
St Lucy (20)		
Agards (by 1891)	5	2 2 00
Allman's (1901)	5	5 0 00
Avice Town (by 1885)	25	15 0 00
Benthams (ditto)	25	10 0 00
Bishops (1875)	5	10 0 00
Cave Hill (by 1901)	10	8 0 00
Connell Town (by 1906)	10	5 0 00
Content (1877)	5	5 0 00
Crab Hill (by 1885)	25	15 0 00
Durhams (by 1875)	6	3 1 00
Free Hill (by 1885)	20	10 0 00
Graveyard (by 1885)	20	15 0 00
Grigg Field (by 1901)	14	1 2 00
Nesfield (by 1885)	5	1 0 00
River Bay (ditto)	5	5 0 00
Roaches (by 1875)	5	5 0 00
Rock Hall (by 1885)	25	15 0 00
Southerland Hill (1889)	6	10 0 00
Spout Farm (by 1885)	25	20 0 00
Swampy Town (by 1918)	5	5 0 00
St Michael (32)		
Armstrong Village (by 1905)	11	6 0 00
Bank Hall Rd (ditto)[4]	7	3 3 00
Bayville/Beckles Rd. (ditto)	10	5 0 00
Nr. Belfield (ditto)	23	10 0 00
Clevedale (by 1900)	20	21 0 00
Danesbury (by 1905)	5	1 2 00
Deacons Rd. (1901)	10	5 0 00
Eagle Hall (by 1905)	10	5 0 00
Eckstein Village (ditto)	12	2 3 00
Flint Hall Gap (by 1900)	14	9 0 00
Free Hill (by 1900)	9	3 3 00

4. The plantation was wholly subdivided after 1914.

Appendix: Free Villages, Number, Approximate Size and Date of Formation

Free Villages	Holdings	Acreage
Government Hill (by 1885)	11	13 0 00
Green Hill (ditto)	25	15 0 00
Halls Rd. (ditto)	25	10 0 00
Hinds Hill/Lodge Hill (by 1895)	17	9 0 00
Howell's Cross Rd. (by 1875)	42	25 0 00
Nr. Husbands (by 1905)	18	14 0 00
The Ivy (by 1900)	20	5 0 00
Licorish Gap (by 1900)	10	6 1 00
Nr. Lodge (by 1885)	19	12 2 00
Lower Birneys (by 1905)	10	5 0 00
The Mount (ditto)	8	11 0 00
Mt. Friendship (by 1875)	22	10 0 00
Ramparts (by 1885)	32	23 1 00
The Rock/Spooners Hill (1875)	9	6 2 00
Rouen (by 1905)	34	12 1 00
Nr. Spring Garden (by 1905)[5]	7	3 2 00
Utility Village (by 1900)	11	5 3 00
Nr. Wanstead (by 1905)	10	6 0 00
Nr. Welches (1905)	10	5 0 00
Westbury Rd. (1905)	9	8 1 00
Woodstock Village (1875)	7	11 1 00
St Peter (7)		
Diamond Corner (by 1885)	30	20 0 00
French Village (by 1906)	10	5 0 00
Indian Ground (by 1918)	10	5 0 00
Lonesome Hill (ditto)	10	5 0 00
Mile and Quarter (by 1885)	35	25 0 0
Retreat (by 1918)	5	2 2 00
Nr. The Risk (by 1876)	5	6 2 00
St Philip (47)		
Nr. Apple Hall (by 1875)	22	33 1 01
Nr. Bayfield (by 1901)	37	47 0 37

5. The plantation was wholly subdivided in the 1920s.

Free Villages	Holdings	Acreage
Nr. Belair (ditto)	5	6 3 21
Blades Hill (by 1875)	38	20 0 15
Nr. Briggs (ditto)	33	25 1 00
Nr. Bushy Park (by 1901)	6	5 3 18
Nr. Cane Garden (1889)	9	3 2 05
Nr. Crane (by 1901)	26	29 1 26
Diamond Valley (by 1895)	9	9 3 16
Downs (by 1901)	11	7 0 14
Draxes/Drakes (by 1875)	13	11 2 21
Nr. Eastbourne (by 1901)	23	23 2 18
Nr. East Point (by 1875)	29	32 0 29
Nr. Ebenezer Church (ditto)	16	12 3 08
Emerton/Blades (ditto)	11	23 0 22
Farm Rd. (ditto)	9	6 3 32
Nr. Fortescue (by 1901)	10	15 0 30
Gibsons & Pinketts (by 1875)	13	9 0 00
Nr. Golden Grove (by 1901)	6	3 3 27
Nr. Grand View (by 1901)	5	4 0 00
Nr. Grove (ditto)	26	20 0 07
Harlington (ditto)	6	4 2 11
Nr. Home (ditto)	11	15 3 09
Nr. Hopeland (by 1875)	25	20 3 34
Nr. Industry Hall (ditto)	13	25 1 08
Jessamine Lane (by 1880)	9	5 1 02
Nr. Jones (by 1901)	8	8 2 34
Nr. Kirtons (ditto)[6]	12	11 2 03
Nr. Loamfield (ditto)	5	4 3 38
Nr. Mangrove (by 1875)	50	37 3 07
Nr. Oldbury (by 1901)	14	6 1 10
Nr. Oughterson (ditto)	5	1 2 15
Nr. Pounders (by 1875)	20	22 2 08
Nr. Rices (by 1901)[7]	13	11 1 04
Nr. Ruby (ditto)	15	12 3 14

6. The plantation, which included Rices, was subdivided in 1912–14.
7. See footnote 6.

Free Villages	Holdings	Acreage
Nr St Martin's Church (by 1875)	31	25 1 05
Nr. Sandford (by 1901)	9	1 2 00
Sandy Hill (ditto)	11	13 1 27
Sea View (by 1875)	8	10 2 18
Six Roads (by 1875)	11	6 1 29
Nr. Spencers (ditto)	9	7 2 23
Stone Hall (by 1901)	7	5 2 23
Nr. Thicket (by 1895)	9	12 2 13
Nr. Union Hall (ditto)	14	21 3 26
Nr. Vineyard (by 1901)	5	2 0 29
Nr. Well House (by 1875)	27	26 2 24
Work Hall (ditto)	18	13 1 18

St Thomas (6)		
Allen View (1881)	12	6 0 00
Arch Hall (by 1875)	10	11 0 00
Arise/Proute's Village (after 1864)	5	10 0 00
Nr. Bagatelle (by 1875)	10	21 2 00
Carrington's Village (ditto)	10	13 0 00
Mess House Hill/ Shop Hill (ditto)	5	5 0 00

Third Phase

Christ Church (26)		
Amity Lodge (by 1917)	9	2 2 22
Belinfante (ditto)	5	10 0 39
Cave Hill (ditto)	8	4 0 02
Chancery Lane (ditto)	47	57 0 19
Charnocks (ditto)	122	141 0 00
Edey's Village (by 1945)	25	27 0 32
Gall Hill (by 1926)	70	35 0 24
Hopewell (by 1917)	86	87 3 19
Industry Hall (by 1945)	5	11 0 00
Kendal Hill (by 1918)	44	24 2 16
Lansdowne (by 1945)	12	9 3 20

Free Villages	Holdings	Acreage
Paradise Village (by 1926)	18	2 0 38
Parish Land (by 1945)	100	73 3 08
Rockley (1924)	67	50 3 05
Rycrofts (by 1917)	17	31 0 00
Sayes Court (1907)	53	32 1 21
Scarborough (by 1917)	25	11 1 05
Sea View (by 1945)	14	7 2 00
Silver Sands (ditto)	28	11 2 10
St. Christopher (ditto)	41	13 2 18
St. Matthias (ditto)	10	2 1 30
Top Rock (ditto)	14	7 1 00
Water Street (ditto)	35	16 2 32
Waverley (ditto)	62	40 1 18
Wilcox (1924)	60	88 3 26
Worthing View (by 1945)	67	39 2 11
St Andrew (8)		
Cane Garden (by 1919)	80	78 1 24
Corbin's Village (by 1939)	18	42 1 29
Indian Ground (by 1945)	7	1 0 04
Licorish Village (ditto)	14	11 0 00
Mango Lodge (ditto)	5	4 0 00
Rock Hall (by 1918)	78	81 1 05
Shorey Village (by 1945)	23	15 0 21
St. Simon's (ditto)	216	154 0 37
St George (14)		
Bridge Cot (1907/08)	85	45 2 24
East Lynne (1917)	51	25 1 37
Ellerton (1911)	193	93 1 29
Foster Lodge (by 1945)	12	6 3 38
Greens (by 1911)	130	97 0 22
Harmony Cottage (ditto)	12	9 1 06
Mayfield (by 1935)	23	13 1 26

Appendix: Free Villages, Number, Approximate Size and Date of Formation

Free Villages	Holdings	Acreage
Paradise Village (by 1945)	14	5 0 00
Parish Land (ditto)	53	15 0 14
Prerogative (by 1924)	57	70 0 26
Salters (by 1929)	141	176 3 30
Superlative (by 1918)	37	28 0 12
Thorpe's Cottage (by 1945)	52	42 0 03
Walker's Valley (ditto)	32	24 2 37
St James (20)		
Cat's Castle (by 1932/3)	6	6 3 25
Dean's Village (by 1918)	9	3 0 00
Derricks (ditto)	29	18 0 06
Durants (ditto)	163	92 3 23
Gilkes Village (ditto)	16	10 3 26
Lower Carlton (ditto)	161	60 3 05
Mount Standfast (ditto)	180	87 2 18
Nicholls' Village (ditto)	21	7 3 00
Porters (by 1945)	13	3 1 00
Reeves Hill (by 1935)	7	4 0 20
Reid's Bay (by 1918)	21	9 0 20
Rock Dundo (1913)	155	73 1 32
Sea View (by 1918)	66	20 0 38
Sion Hill (1913)	48	27 1 18
Thorpes (by 1918)	56	28 1 18
Upper Carlton (ditto)	143	66 0 20
Waterman's (ditto)	16	5 1 29
Westmoreland (by 1945)	87	49 0 29
Weston (by 1918)	144	80 0 10
Whapping (ditto)	49	14 1 14
St John (19)		
Carters (by 1916)	32	20 0 05
Cheshire (ditto)	16	5 3 36
Church View (by 1945)	8	5 1 00

Free Villages	Holdings	Acreage
Clarke's Land (ditto)	8	6 1 03
Cliff Cottage (by 1916)	38	14 1 18
Edge Cliff (by 1945)	54	27 3 37
Four Cross Rds. (by 1916)	5	2 2 30
Glebe Land (by 1945)	28	15 0 00
Howard's Hill (by 1916)	6	1 2 20
Humphrey's Hill (ditto)	6	4 2 21
Knight's Village (by 1916)	7	3 0 22
Millers Land (by 1945)	6	15 2 00
Mt. Pleasant (ditto)	8	7 3 00
Roebuck St. (by 1916)	5	1 3 38
Sealy Hall (ditto)	44	36 2 20
Sherbourne (by 1929)	88	47 0 29
Small Town (by 1916)	5	1 2 00
Venture (by 1913)	101	71 3 21
Welch Town (by 1945)	13	17 3 03
St Joseph (9)		
Airy Hill (by 1916)	56	33 1 34
Chimborazo (1909/20)	48	33 0 38
Church Village (by 1945)	23	14 3 08
Clement Rock (by 1916)	10	8 1 00
Horse Hill (by 1945)	15	9 0 24
Mt. Dacres (by 1916)	14	18 3 21
Overton's (by 1945)	11	5 1 24
Union (by 1916)	15	9 1 32
Vaughans Land (by 1921)	25	17 0 00
St Lucy (35)		
Air View (1906/07)	6	4 3 05
Alexandria (by 1945)	64	38 0 08
Archers (by 1918)	6	3 3 21

Appendix: Free Villages, Number, Approximate Size and Date of Formation

Free Villages	Holdings	Acreage
Cave (ditto)	5	2 2 20
Chance Hall (by 1913)	68	75 0 08
Checker Hall (by1918)	198	185 1 04
Clinketts (ditto)	7	1 2 29
Coconut Tree Hall (ditto)	9	9 3 21
Cole's Cave (ditto)	11	5 2 30
Crick (by 1945)	5	3 1 00
Elcocks (by 1918)	9	9 2 34
Fustic (by 1918)	43	14 1 36
Gilkes (ditto)	19	6 3 02
Glendlebrough (ditto)	28	16 0 6
Grape Hall (ditto)	36	18 0 16
Half Moon Fort (ditto)	34	14 2 38
Halls (ditto)	7	9 3 19
Harrises (ditto)	30	8 2 06
Higginsons (ditto)	9	12 3 29
Hope Rd. & Bridge (ditto)	90	47 0 01
Jordans (by 1945)	23	13 3 16
Less Beholden (by 1945)	32	18 1 28
Lowlands (ditto)	9	5 2 00
Lyder Cottage (ditto)	16	3 2 04
McClean's (ditto)	9	4 2 00
Mt. Johnson (ditto)	18	9 3 05
Mt. View (by 1918)	40	36 2 06
Petersys (by 1945)	18	12 3 16
Retreat (by 1918)	35	25 0 38
The Risk (by 1945)	10	6 0 36
Rockfield (1907)	43	42 3 18
Salmonds (by 1918)	47	48 3 37
Shermans (by 1945)	20	5 2 16
Wakenham (by 1918)	5	4 2 36
Wellfield (ditto)	25	16 3 32

Free Villages	Holdings	Acreage
St Michael (16)		
Bank Hall (by 1914)	124	34 3 34
Bush Hall (by 1933)	351	94 3 16
Clapham (by 1918)	95	73 1 08
Deighton's Rd. (by 1945)	15	3 0 38
Fairfield & Tudor Bridge (by 1929)	154	68 0 22
Gilkes' Village (by 1945)	32	10 1 14
Goodland (by 1928)	214	48 2 27
Grazettes (by 1937)	45	12 0 08
Haggatt Hall (by 1945)	257	259 0 21
Jack ma' nanny Gap/Wavell Ave. (by 1920)	106	36 3 21
Jackman's (by 1917/18)	168	136 2 36
Jackson's (ditto)	190	126 0 35
Lazaretto (by 1945)	6	7 1 00
Lower Birneys (1917/18)	56	33 0 02
Piper's Hill (by 1945)	8	3 3 19
Whitehall (by 1918)	147	110 0 06
St Peter (13)		
Ashton Hall (1932)	226	167 3 15
Battaleys (by 1918)	26	10 2 32
Bowling Alley (ditto)	13	5 2 06
Nr. Castle (ditto)	6	7 1 00
Date Tree Hill (ditto)	17	6 0 36
Farm Rd. & Tenantry (by 1916)	127	44 3 38
Newstead (by 1945)	15	4 0 17
Queen St. (ditto)	26	11 0 18
Road View (by 1918)	33	17 1 29
Rose Hill (by 1945)	7	2 3 00
Shermans (by 1919)	10	3 3 13
Sunbury (by 1918)	10	11 0 00
The Whim (ditto)	86	48 1 38

Appendix: Free Villages, Number, Approximate Size and Date of Formation 125

Free Villages	Holdings	Acreage
St Philip (13)		
Clarke's/nr. Home (by 1945)	27	33 1 20
Content Cot (by 1911)	7	10 3 38
Cottage Vale (ditto)	17	25 1 30
Diamond (by 1945)	21	17 0 13
Four Roads (by 1920)	14	12 1 20
Nr. Hampden (by 1915)	18	12 2 27
Heddings (by 1920)	6	8 3 00
Highlands (by 1945)	17	11 3 00
Kirtons (by 1920)	190	221 2 21
Marchfield (by 1910)	155	108 0 14
Roses (by 1920)	12	12 1 00
Stroude's Land (by 1915)	25	14 3 02
Woodbourne (by 1917)	21	12 2 02

Free Villages	Holdings	Acreage
St Thomas (10)		
Airy Cot (by 1945)	13	10 0 13
Apple Grove (ditto)	6	7 0 00
Arthur Seat (by 1918)	141	92 0 32
Hillaby (1913–29)	43	26 0 38
Jackson (by 1945)	31	16 0 22
Kew Land (by 1918)	8	3 2 00
Melrose/Shorey Village (ditto)	41	26 1 34
Padmore Village (ditto)	8	4 0 11
Spring Farm (by 1935)	49	37 2 34
Welchman Hall (by 1927)	156	155 2 31

Bibliography

Primary Sources (*in Barbados Department of Archives or otherwise located*)
Instructions to Stipendiary Magistrates, 1842 (*Parliamentary Papers* 1842, vol.13, Appendix)
Police Magistrates' Reports to Colonial Office, 1838-42
List of Landowners of one acre and upwards, 1847
Parish Rate Books, 1852-1941
Reports on Censuses, 1851-1921
Voters' Lists
Return of Persons liable to Militia Tax, 1875
Listing of Principal Villages, 1885 (from Report of Water Supply Commission)
Report of West India Royal Commission, 1897
List of contract workers bound for Panama 1906-7
CC Skeete's *The Condition of Peasant Agriculture in Barbados*, 1930
Report of the West India Sugar Commission, 1930
Report on the Barbados Disturbances, 1937
Report of West India Royal Commission, 1945
West Indian Agricultural Census, 1946
M Halcrow and JM Cave: *Peasant Agriculture in Barbados*, 1947

Newspapers
Very limited information was provided by:
Barbadian (violently opposed)
West Indian
Liberal (fully supportive)
Agricultural Reporter (also violently opposed)
Barbados Advocate (holding middle ground)

Pre-1945 Sources
Barratt, John. Letter of 27 Oct. 1857 to Methodist Missionary Society.

Bell, Gordon, writing as George Bernard *Wayside Sketches, Pen Pictures of Barbadian Life*. Barbados, 1934. Republished in 1985 by Nation Publishing Co. Ltd.

Davy, John. *The West Indies, Before and Since Slave Emancipation*. London: Cass, 1971 (1854).

Dodsworth, Francis. *Book of the West Indies*. London: Routledge, 1904.

Edghill, James Young. *About Barbados*. London: C. Tallis, 1890.

Hinton, J.H. *Memoir of William Knibb, Missionary in Jamaica*. Houlston and London: Stoneman, 1847.

Leverick, Percy. *Leverick's Directory of Barbados, 1921*.

McLellan, George. *Some Phases of Barbadian Life: Tropical Scenes and Studies*, Georgetown: Argosy Co, Ltd, 1909.

Merivale, Herman. *Lectures on Colonization and Colonies*. London: Longman, Green, Longman and Roberts, 1841, 1861. Reprinted in 1967 by Augustus Kelley, New York.

Philippo, J.M. *Jamaica: Its Past and Present State*. London: John Snow, 1843.

Schomburgk, R.T. *The History of Barbados*. London: Longmans, 1848. Frank Cass Reprint 1971.

Sewell, W.G. (1862), *The Ordeal of Free Labour in the British West Indies*, reprint Frank Cass, 1968

Sinckler, E.G. *The Barbados Handbook 1913*. London: Duckworth, 1913.

Starkey, O.P. *The Economic Geography of* Barbados. New York: Columbia University Press, 1939.

Thome, James, and J.H. Kimball (1838), *Emancipation in the West Indies. A Six Months' Tour*. New York: Arno Press & New York Times, 1838, reprint 1969.

Vaughan, H.A. "Some Social and Political Tendencies, 1910–1935." *Silver Jubilee Magazine* 1935.

Wickham, Clennell C. *Pen and Ink Sketches and Other Essays of Barbadian Politicians*. Bridgetown: *Barbados Herald*, 1921. Reprinted as *Man with a Fountain Pen*, Nation Publishing Co., 1995.

Wrong, Hume. *Government of the West Indies*. Oxford: Oxford University Press, 1923.

Modern Works

Adamson, A.H. *Sugar Without Slaves: The Political Economy of British Guiana, 1838–1904*. New Haven: Yale University Press, 1972.

Barrow, Christine. "Reputation and Ranking in a Barbadian Locality." *Social and Economic Studies* 25, no. 2 (1976): 106–21.

Beachey, R.W. *The British West Indies Sugar Industry in the late 19th Century*. Oxford: Blackwell, 1957.

Beckles, H. McD. *A History of Barbados from Amerindian Settlement to Caribbean Single Market*. Cambridge: Cambridge University Press, 1990.
Besson, Jean. *Martha Brae's Two Histories*. Kingston: Ian Randle Publishers, 2002.
Brereton, Bridget. *Race Relations in Trinidad, 1870-1900*. Cambridge: Cambridge University Press, 1979.
Braithwaite, Lloyd. "Social and Political Aspects of Rural Development in the West Indies." *Social and Economic Studies* 17, no. 3 (1968): 264-75.
Browne, David. *Race, Class, Politics and the Struggle for Empowerment in Barbados, 1914-1937*. Kingston: Ian Randle Publishers, 2012.
Campbell, P.F. *Some Early Barbadian History*. Bridgetown, Barbados, 1990.
Carnegie, C.V., ed. *Afro-Caribbean Villages in Historical Perspective*. Kingston: African-Caribbean Institute of Jamaica, 1987.
Carter, Henderson. *Labour Pains: Resistance and Protest in Barbados 1838-1904*. Kingston: Ian Randle Publishers, 2012.
Chamberlain, Mary. "Renters and Farmers: the Barbadian Plantation Tenantry System, 1917-1937." *Journal of Caribbean History* 24, no. 2 (1990): 195-225.
Clarke, Edith. *My Mother Who Fathered Me: A Study of the Family in Three Selected Communities in Jamaica*. London: Allen & Unwin, 1957.
Cox, Martin. "The Founding of Shorey's Village and the Shoreys." *Journal of the Barbados Museum and Historical Society (JBMHS)* 69 (2023): 27-54.
Craig-James, Susan. *The Changing Society of Tobago, 1838-1938: A Fractured Whole*, 2 vols. Arima, Trinidad: Cornerstone Press, 2008.
Craton, Michael. "Reshuffling the Pack: The Transition from Slavery to Other Forms of Labour in the British Caribbean, ca. 1790-1890." *New West Indian Guide* 68, nos. 1&2 (1994): 23-75.
Crichlow, Michaeline. "An Alternative approach to Family Land Tenure in the Anglophone Caribbean: The Case of St Lucia." *New West Indian Guide* 68, nos. 1&2 (1994): 77-99.
Cumper, George. "A Modern Jamaican Sugar Estate." *Social and Economic Studies* 3, no. 2 (1954): 119-60.
Downes, Aviston. "Panama Money: General Effects." In *The Barbados-Panama Connection Revisited*, edited by Velma Newton et al., 121-44. Bridgetown: Barbados Museum & Historical Society, 2014.
Dunn, Richard S. *Sugar and Slaves: The Rise of the Planter Class in the English West Indies, 1624-1713*. Chapel Hill: University of North Carolina Press, 1972.

Eisner, Gisela. *Jamaica, 1830-1930: A Study in Economic Growth*. Manchester: Manchester University Press, 1961.

Farley, Rawle. "The Rise of Village Settlements in British Guiana." *Caribbean Quarterly* 10.1 (1964): 52-61

Franklin, Ann. "Mount Clapham: Plantation to Village." Caribbean Study submitted at Cave Hill, University of the West Indies, 1981.

Gibbs, Bentley. "The Establishment of the Tenantry System in Barbados." In *Emancipation II*, edited by Woodville Marshall, 23-45. Department of History, University of the West Indies, Cave Hill, 1987.

Gmelch, George, and Sharon Gmelch. *The Parish behind God's Back*. Ann Arbor: University of Michigan Press, 1997.

Green, W.A. *British Slave Emancipation: The Sugar Colonies and the Great Experiment, 1830-1865*. Oxford: Clarendon Press, 1976.

Greenfield, Sidney. "Land Tenure and Transmission in Rural Barbados." *Anthropological Quarterly* 33 (1960): 165-76.

Greenfield, Sidney. *English Rustics in Black Skin: A Study of Modern Family Forms in a Pre-industrialised Society*. New Haven: College and University Press, 1966.

Hall, Catherine. *Civilising Subjects: Metropole and Colony in the English Imagination 1830-1867*. Chicago and London: University of Chicago Press, 2002.

Hall, Douglas. *Free Jamaica 1838-1865: An Economic History*. New Haven: Yale University Press, 1959.

Hamilton, Bruce. *Barbados & the Confederation Question, 1871-1885*, London: Crown Agents, 1956.

Henshall, Janet. "Post-Emancipation Rural Settlement in the Lesser Antilles." *Proceedings of the Association of American Geographers* 8 (1976): 37-40.

Herskovits, M.J., and Frances S. Herskovits. *Trinidad Village*. New York: Knopf, 1974.

Higman, B.W. *Montpelier Jamaica: A Plantation Community in Slavery and Freedom 1739-1912*. Kingston: University of the West Indies Press, 1998.

Holt, T.C. *The Problem of Freedom: Race and Labour in Jamaica and Britain, 1832-1938*. Baltimore: Johns Hopkins University Press, 1992.

Hughes, Ronald. "Jacob Hinds, White Father of a Mulatto Clan." *JBMHS* (2006): 12-16.

———. "Sweet Bottom, St George, Barbados: An Early (1777) Non-White Freehold Village." *JBMHS* 36, no. 3 (1979): 266-76.

Karch, Cecilia with Henderson Carter. *The Rise of the Phoenix: The Barbados Mutual Life Assurance in Caribbean Economy and Society, 1840-1990*. Kingston: Ian Randle Publishers, 1997.
Lewis, Kingsley. *The Moravian Mission in Barbados 1816-1886*. Peter Lang, Frankfurt, 1985.
Levy, Claude. *Emancipation, Sugar, and Federalism: Barbados and the West Indies, 1833-1876*. Gainesville: University Presses of Florida, 1980.
Lowenthal, David. "The Population of Barbados." in *Social and Economic Studies* 6, no. 4 (1975): 445-501.
Marshall, Sharon Milagro. *Tell My Mother I Gone to Cuba: Stories of Early Twentieth Century Migration from Barbados*. Kingston: University of the West Indies Press, 2016.
Marshall, Woodville. "Aspects of the Development of the Peasantry." *Caribbean Quarterly* 18, no. 1 (1972): 39-46.
Marshall, Woodville. "List of Voters 1873: A Comment." *JBMHS* 51 (2005): 187-241.
Marshall, Woodville. "Rock Hall, St Thomas, A Free Village in Barbados." *Journal of Caribbean History (JCH)* 41, nos. 1&2 (2007): 1-50.
Marshall, Woodville. "Routes to Chattel Village: Bequest and Family Villages in Post-Slavery Barbados." *JCH* 48, nos. 1&2 (2014): 86-107.
Marshall, Woodville. "'Designing' Individual or 'Celebrated Solicitor'? Peter Chapman's Activity and Role as Land Speculator after Emancipation." *JBMHS* 63 (2017): 6-31.
Marshall, Woodville. "Remittance Villages in Barbados, c. 1905-c. 1935." *JCH* 54, no. 2 (2000): 211-27.
———. et al. "The Establishment of a Peasantry in Barbados, 1840-1920." In *Social Groups and Institutions in the History of the Caribbean*, edited by Thomas Matthews, 85-104. Rio Piedras, Puerto Rico: Association of Caribbean Historians, 1975.
Mintz, S.W. *Caribbean Transformations*. Chicago: Aldine Press, 1974.
———. "From Plantations to Peasantries in the Caribbean." In *Caribbean Contours*, edited by S.W. Mintz and Sally Price, 127-53. Baltimore: Johns Hopkins University Press, 1985.
———. "Historical Sociology of the Jamaican Church-Founded Free Village System." *De West-Indische Gids* 38, nos. 1&2 (1958): 46-70.
———. "Slavery and the Rise of Peasantries." In *Roots and Branches: Current Directions in Slavery Studies*, edited by Michael Craton, 213-42. Toronto: Pergamon Press, 1979.

Momsen, Janet Henshall. "Caribbean Peasantry Revisited: Barbadian Farmers over Four Decades." *Southeastern Geographer* 45, no. 2 (2005): 206–21.

Moore, Brian. *Race, Power and Social Segmentation in Colonial Society: Guyana after Slavery 1838–1891.* New York and London: Gordon and Breach, 1987.

Newton, Melanie. *Children of Africa in the Colonies: Free People of Colour in Barbados in the Age of Emancipation.* Baton Rouge: Louisiana State University Press, 2008.

Newton, Velma. *The Silver Men: West Indian Labour Migration to Panama 1850–1914.* Kingston: Ian Randle Publishers, 1984, 2004.

Paget, Hugh. "The Free Village System in Jamaica." *Caribbean Quarterly* 1, no. 4 (1954): 38–51.

Richardson, B.C. *Economy and Environment: Barbados and the Windwards in the Late 1880s.* Kingston and Gainesville: University of the West Indies Press and University Press of Florida, 1997.

———. "Livelihood in Rural Trinidad in 1900." *Annals of the Association of American Geographers* 65, no. 2 (1975): 240–51.

———. *Panama Money in Barbados, 1900–1920.* Knoxville: University of Tennessee Press, 1985.

———. "Plantation and Village in Coastal Guyana, 1887–1969: Conflict or Complementarity?" *Journal of Historical Geography* 3, no. 4 (1977): 349–62.

———. "Plantation Infrastructure and Labour Mobility in Guyana and Trinidad." In *Migration and Development*, edited by Helen Safa and Brian Du Toit, 205–24. The Hague: Mouton Publishers, 1975.

Roberts, G.W. "Emigration from the Island of Barbados." *Social and Economic Studies* 4, no. 3 (1955): 245–87.

Rodney, Walter. *A History of the Guyanese Working Class People, 1881–1905.* London: Heinemann, 1981.

Satchell, Veront. *From Plots to Plantations: Land Transactions in Jamaica, 1866–1900.* Kingston: Institute of Social and Economic Studies, University of the West Indies, 1990.

———. "Squatters or Freeholders? The Case of the Jamaican Peasants during the Mid-nineteenth Century." *Journal of Caribbean History* 23, no. 2 (1989): 164–77.

Sebastien, Raphael. "A Typology of the Caribbean Peasantry – The Development of the Peasantry in Trinidad, 1845–1917." In *Social and Economic Studies* 29, nos. 2&3 (1980): 109–33.

Senior, Olive. *Dying to Better Themselves: West Indians and the Building of the Panama Canal.* Kingston: University of the West Indies Press, 2014.

Sheppard, Jill., *The "Redlegs" of Barbados: Their Origins and History.* Millwood, NY: KTO Press, 1977.

Slocum, Karla. "Caribbean Free Villages: Towards an Anthropology of Blackness, Place, and Freedom." *American Ethnologist* 44, no. 3 (2017): 425-34.

Smith, M.G. *Kinship & Community in Carriacou.* New Haven: Yale University Press, 1962.

Smith, R.T. *The Negro Family in British Guiana: Family Structure and Social Status in the Villages.* London: Routledge & Kegan Paul, 1956.

Stafford, Patricia. "A Barbados Museum Founding Father: James Christopher Lynch and his Fascinating Family History." *JBMHS* 56 (2010): 62-73.

———. "Death of a Plantation, Growth of a Community: Goodland, St Michael, 1900-1960." *JBMHS* 49 (2003): 204-18.

Sutton, Constance. "The Scene of the Action: A Wildcat Strike in Barbados." Doctoral dissertation, Columbia University, 1969.

Taitt, Etheline. "Chimborazo." Caribbean Study submitted at the University of the West Indies, Cave Hill, Barbados, 1982.

Trouillot, Michel-Rolph. "Beyond and Below the Merivale Paradigm: Dominica, the First 100 Days of Freedom." In *The Lesser Antilles in the Age of European Expansion*, edited by R.L. Paquette and S.L. Engerman, 305-23. Gainesville: University Press of Florida, 1996.

———. *Peasants and Capital: Dominica in the World Economy.* Baltimore: Johns Hopkins University Press, 1988.

Vernon, K.C., and D.M. Carroll. *Soil and Land Use Surveys No. 18 Barbados.* Faculty of Agriculture, University of the West Indies, St Augustine, Trinidad, 1966.

Watson, Karl. "Bridgetown Expands in the late Nineteenth Century: The Creation of the Suburbs of Belleville and Strathclyde." *JBMHS* 49 (2003): 192-203.

Watts, D. "Man's Influence on the Vegetation of Barbados, 1627-1800." In *University of Hull Occasional Papers in Geography* 4 (1966): 1-96.

———. *The West Indies: Patterns of Development, Culture and Environmental Change since 1492.* Cambridge: Cambridge University Press, 1987.

Wilmot, S.R. "Politics at the 'Grassroots' in Free Jamaica: St James 1838 Working Slavery, Pricing Freedom: Perspectives from the Caribbean, Africa and the African Diaspora 1865." In *Working Slavery, Pricing Freedom: Perspectives from the Caribbean, Africa and the African Diaspora*, edited by Verene Shepherd, 449-66. Kingston: Ian Randle Publishers, 2002.

———. "'A Stake in the Soil': Land and Creole Politics in Free Jamaica, the 1849 Elections." In *In the Shadow of the Plantation*, edited by Alvin Thompson, 314–33. Kingston: Ian Randle Publishers, 2002.

Wood, Donald. *Trinidad in Transition: The Years after Slavery*. Oxford: Oxford University Press, 1968.

Young, Allan. *Approaches to Local Self-Government*. London: Longmans Green, 1958.

Index

a denotes Appendix; *f* denotes a figure; *n* denotes an endnote; *t* denotes a table

(The) Abbey, Christ Church parish, size and date of formation for, 112*a*
Above the Second High Cliff, sparse free village settlement on, 28
Adams Castle, Christ Church parish, size and date of formation for, 112*a*
Adamson, Alan, 2
Adams, Grantley Herbert, 99
Advocate (Barbados newspaper), 71, 77. See also *Barbados Advocate*
African and Africa-descended population, 17
Agards, St Lucy parish, size and date of formation for, 116*a*
Agricultural Aids Act, 70
agricultural labourers, villagers and, 65
Agricultural Reporter (Barbados newspaper), 71; on election upset of 1865, 97; on subdivision of plantation lands, 77

Airy Cot, St Thomas parish, size and date of formation for, 125*a*
Airy Hill, St George parish, 62–63; developed via land speculator Chapman, 44; early farming lots established, 26; registered voters in 1870s in, 96; size and date of formation for, 110*a*; uniquely large size of, 45
Airy Hill, St Joseph parish, 83–84; size and date of formation for, 122*a*
Airy Hill, St Philip parish, 35
Air View, St Lucy parish, size and date of formation for, 122*a*
Alexandria, St Lucy parish, 81; size and date of formation for, 122*a*
Allen View, St Thomas parish, size and date of formation for, 119*a*
Alleyne, Charles, 60
Allman's, St Lucy parish, size and date of formation for, 116*a*
Amity Lodge, Christ Church parish, size and date of formation for, 119*a*

Anglican churches, Barbadian villages around, 30
annuities paid to labourers, 39
anti-immigration: stance held by planters, 21; relaxation of, 55
Anti-Slavery Reporter, 22
Apple Grove, Christ Church parish, size and date of formation for, 109*a*
Appleby Gardens, St James parish: registered voters in 1870s in, 96; size and date of formation for, 114*a*
Apple Grove, St Thomas parish, size and date of formation for, 125*a*
apprenticeship period, legislature passed during, 20
arable land, appropriation of, 17
Arch Hall, St Thomas parish, size and date of formation for, 119*a*
Archers, St Lucy parish, size and date of formation for, 122*a*
Arise/Proute's Village, St Thomas parish, 54; size and date of formation for, 119*a*
Armstrong Village, St Michael parish, size and date of formation for, 116*a*
Arthur Seat, St Thomas parish, size and date of formation for, 125*a*
Arthur Seat plantation, St Thomas parish, 83
artisans, villagers as, 65

Ashton Hall plantation, St Peter parish, 82; size and date of formation for, 124*a*
Austin, C. Miller, 72
Avis (Avice) Town, St Lucy parish, 53; size and date of formation for, 116*a*

Back River, St Andrew parish, size and date of formation for, 113*a*
Baeza, Edmund (land speculator), 75, 80
Baeza, Joshua (land speculator), 75, 80
Baird's Village, St George parish, size and date of formation for, 113*a*
Bank Hall, St Michael parish, size and date of formation for, 124*a*
Bank Hall Rd, St Michael parish, size and date of formation for, 116*a*
Barbadian (newspaper), letter belittling the smallholder vote in the, 41
Barbadian free village development, characteristics of a, 40
Barbados: Annual Reports of 1848 and 1858, 24; African descendants on, 17; election of 1848, 40–41; lack of arable land for freedmen and women, 24; price of land, 23; post-slavery social developments in, 1; population density of, 17; record-keeping in, 10

Barbados Advocate (newspaper), 103*n*15; as source of information on free village development, 8. See also *Advocate*
Barbados Savings Bank, 95
Barrow, Christine, 9
Bartletts, Christ Church parish, size and date of formation for, 112*a*
Bascom, James Sarsfield, 41
Bath Village, Christ Church parish, 34
Batson, Robert Hudgwell, will of, 34
Battaleys plantation, St Peter parish, 82; size and date of formation for, 124*a*
Bay Land (Bay Ville), St Michael parish, growth of during first phase, 88
Bayley, Haynes, 41
Baylcy, Joseph, 39, 40, 43*t*, 39, 72
Bayville/Beckles Rd., St Michael parish, size and date of formation for, 116*a*
Baywoods, St James parish, size and date of formation for, 114*a*
Beckles, Hilary, 89–90
beet sugar, 11; crisis due to, 55, 60, 61; abolition of bounties, 70; as cause of depression in sugar industry, 69
Belinfante, Christ Church parish, size and date of formation for, 119*a*
Belle Gully, St Michael parish: size and date of formation for, 111*a;* size of small holdings in, 27
Belleplaine, St Andrew parish: growth of during first phase, 88; as a large village, 54; size and date of formation for, 113*a*
Belleville, 58
Below Almshouse, St George parish, size and date of formation for, 113*a*
Below the Cliff, sparse free village settlement on, 15
Below the First High Cliff, free villages located in, 28
Below the Second High Cliff, sparse free village settlement on, 28
Below the Rock: poor white settlement at, 17; sparse free village settlement on, 15
Benjamin (son of John Christopher Douglin), 32
Benthams, St Lucy parish, 53; size and date of formation for, 116*a*
Bequest Village, St Philip parish, 34–35; size and date of formation for, 111*a*
bequests of land, general type, 31, 35–37, 88
bequests of land, third type (to all enslaved adults), 35–36
bequests of land, in-family (legitimate family) type, 31–33; and division of small property, 64
bequests of land, outside family type, 31, 34–35

bequests of land and free villages, 30–37; definition of and types of, 31; number and size of, 36*t*; decrease of during second phase, 57
Besson, Jean, 1, 31
Bibby's Lane (Near Lears), St Michael parish, 63; intensification process at, 64; size and date of formation for, 111*a*
Birketts, Christ Church parish, size and date of formation for, 109*a*
Bishops, St Lucy parish, size and date of formation for, 116*a*
Blackrock, St Michael parish, 28, 29, 30, 56, 63; growth of during first phase, 88; size and date of formation for, 111*a*; size of small holdings in, 28; villages formed along corridors, 64
black community: Chapman viewed favourably by the, 46; demand for land by, 59–60, 76; practising their version of land bequests, 64; settlement pattern changed from 1840 to 20th century for the, 84
Blades, Robert Doughty, 58
Blades Hill, Christ Church parish, a principal village, 52
Blades Hill, St Philip parish, size and date of formation for, 118*a*

Blair, Mary Catherine, 34
Bonwell, St Joseph parish, size and date of formation for, 115*a*
Boscobel, St Andrew parish: registered voters in 1870s in, 96; size and date of formation for, 113*a*
Boscobel plantation, Potato Riot at, 89, 89
bottom tier parishes, 50, 54
Bourne Village/Cole Hole, St George parish, size and date of formation for, 113*a*
Bournes, Christ Church parish, size and date of formation for, 109*a*
Bowen, William Johnson, 32
Bowling Alley, St Joseph parish, 53; size and date of formation for, 115*a*
Bowling Alley, St Peter parish, size and date of formation for, 124*a*
Boyce, E.P., 74
Braggs Hill, St Joseph parish, 53; size and date of formation for, 115*a*
Branchberry, St Joseph parish, 53; size and date of formation for, 115*a*
Brathwaite, Chrissie, 99
Brathwaite, Edward, 32
Brathwaite, Margaret, 32
Brathwaite, Moses, 32
Braithwaite, Samuel, 32
Breedys, Christ Church parish, size and date of formation for, 112*a*

Brereton, St Philip parish, size and date of formation for, 111*a*
Briar Hall, Christ Church parish, size and date of formation for, 112*a*
Bridge, St Lucy parish, 81
Bridge Cot, St George parish, size and date of formation for, 120*a*
Bridgefield, St Thomas parish, 1; land acquired through communal action, 37; early farming lots established, 26; established as a free village, 38; founders of, 90; size and date of formation for, 111*a*
Bridgetown, 79; black Barbadians residing in, 84; internal migration to, 29
Bridgetown district, St Michael parish, 79
Briggs, Augustus, 97
Briggs Hill, St George parish, size and date of formation for, 114*a*
Bright Hill, Christ Church parish, size and date of formation for, 109*a*
Bright Hill plantation, 33
British Caribbean, 1
British government, plea for relief by, 61
British Guiana, 37
Brittons Hill, St Michael parish, 56; size and date of formation for, 111*a;* villages formed along corridors, 64
Browne, Samuel (land speculator), 72, 82

Brown's Bay, Christ Church parish, size and date of formation for, 112*a*
Burke's Land, an example of a mini-village, 64
Burnetts, Christ Church parish, size and date of formation for, 112*a*
Bush Hall, St Michael parish, large size of, 79; size and date of formation for, 124*a*

Cambridge, St Joseph parish, size and date of formation for, 115*a*
Campion/Campaign Castle, St George parish: developed via land speculator Chapman, 44; size and date of formation for, 110*a*
Cane Garden, St Andrew parish, 59, 83; size and date of formation for, 120*a*
Cane Hill, St George parish registered voters in 1870s in, 96; size and date of formation for, 110*a*
cane sugar. *See* sugar cane; sugar cane industry
Cane Valley, Christ Church parish, size and date of formation for, 109*a*
Carrington's Village, St Thomas parish, 58; registered voters in 1870s in, 96; size and date of formation for, 119*a*
Carter, Henderson, 2, 22, 98
Carters, St John parish, size and date of formation for, 121*a*
Cat's Castle, St James parish,

size and date of formation for, 121*a*
Cave, J.M. *See* Halcrow, M. and J.M. Cave
Cave, St Lucy parish, size and date of formation for, 123*a*
Cave Hill, Christ Church parish, size and date of formation for, 119*a*
Cave Hill, St Lucy parish, size and date of formation for, 116*a*
Cave Hill/Rock Dundo village, St Michael parish, 43; registered voters in 1870s in, 96; size and date of formation for, 111*a*
censuses, as source of information on development of free villages, 8
Chamberlain, Mary, 100
Chance Hall, St Lucy parish, 81; size and date of formation for, 123*a*
Chancery Lane, Christ Church parish, 74; size and date of formation for, 119*a*
Chapel Hill, St Michael parish, 63
Chapman, Peter, 24–25, 26, 43, 43*t*, 48; comparison to Charles Joseph Greenidge, 58; established "farming lots" at Airy Hill, 62–63; land sales resulting in free villages, 43–46; replicated village formation as occurred at Rock Hall village, 40

"Chapman" villages, 44–45
Chapman's Village, St Thomas parish, size and date of formation for, 111*a*
charity, as catalyst for free village development, 54
Charles Rowe Village, St George parish, size and date of formation for, 114*a*
Charnocks, Christ Church parish, size and date of formation for, 119*a*
Charnocks plantation, 75; subdivided by the Baeza brothers, 80
Checker Hall, St Lucy parish, 81; conversion of farming lots to house-spots, 84–85; size and date of formation for, 123*a*
Cheltenham, St Andrew parish, size and date of formation for, 109*a*
Cherry Grove, St John parish, 43; registered voters in 1870s in, 96; size and date of formation for, 110*a*
Cheshire, St John parish, size and date of formation for, 121*a*
Chimborazo plantation, St Joseph parish, 75
Chimborazo, St Joseph parish, size and date of formation for, 122*a*
cholera pandemic, 55
Christ Church parish, 7, 26; bequests of land through in-family transfer, 31; distribution of villages

according to number of holdings within villages, 51*t*; environmental features of high-density free villages in, 78–79; expansion of free villages in, 50–51, 52; first free villages listed by number, type and size in, 28*t*; as a first tier parish, 50–52; free villages on marginal lands of, 28; high concentration of free villages in, 87; holdings in third phase villages in, 78*t*, 80; number, size, and date of formation of villages in, 109*a*, 112*a*–113*a*, 119*a*–120*a*; number and size of bequest villages in, 36*t*; number of villages, holdings and acreage (1905–45), 67*t*; pre-emancipation villages in, 19*t*; rural to urban migration, 64; settlement patterns altered during third phase of development seen in, 84; size of holdings in, 85; suburban expansion in, 56; tally of free villages in, 86*t*; villages formed through land bequests, 34
Christ Church Ridge, free villages located in, 28
Christie, George, will of, 57
Christie's Village, St Thomas parish, 57
church/missionary sponsorship, lack of in Barbados, 30
Church View, St John parish, size and date of formation for, 121*a*
Church Village, St Joseph parish: poor white settlement at, 17; size and date of formation for, 122*a*
civil registration records, as source of information on free village development, 6–7
Clapham, St Michael parish, size and date of formation for, 124*a*
Clarke, Edith, 31
Clarke, Louis Whitfield, 75
Clarke, William, 58
Clarke's Hill, St Philip parish, 58
Clarke's Land, St John parish, size and date of formation for, 122*a*
Clarke's/Near Home, St Philip parish, size and date of formation for, 125*a*
Clement Rock, St Joseph parish, size and date of formation for, 122*a*
Clevedale, St Michael parish, size and date of formation for, 116*a*
Cliff Cottage, St John parish, size and date of formation for, 122*a*
Cliff Cottage, St John parish, 83
Clinketts, St Lucy parish, size and date of formation for, 123*a*
cluster communities, 13
Coach Hill, St John parish: as a principal village, 54; size

and date of formation for, 115*a*
Cocoanut Grove, St Joseph parish, size and date of formation for, 115*a*
Cocoanut Tree Hall, St Lucy parish, size and date of formation for, 123*a*
Cocoanut Walk, Christ Church parish, size and date of formation for, 112*a*
Codrington Hill, St Michael parish, 28, 29, 56; size and date of formation for, 111*a;* size of small holdings in, 27; villages formed along corridors, 64
Coffee Gully, St Joseph parish, size and date of formation for, 115*a*
Cole Hole, St George parish, 53
Cole's Cave, St Lucy parish, size and date of formation for, 123*a*
Collymore Rock, St Michael parish, 56; size and date of formation for, 111*a;* villages formed along corridors, 64
Colonial Office, 30; monitoring of labour situation by the, 3–4
Commercial Crisis of 1847, 55
communal action: land transfer through, 37–38; not strong in Barbados, 30
(The) Condition of Peasant Agriculture in Barbados (Skeete, 1930), 5
Connell Town, St Lucy parish, size and date of formation for, 116*a*

Content, St Lucy parish, size and date of formation for, 116*a*
Content/Bermuda Land, St Michael parish, developed via land speculator Chapman, 44
Content Cot, St Philip parish, size and date of formation for, 125*a*
controverted elections, 96–97
Controverted Election of 1849, 40
Corbin's Village, St Andrew parish, size and date of formation for, 120*a*
Cottage Vale, St Philip parish, size and date of formation for, 125*a*
Court of Chancery, 62, 70, 73; on subdividing indebted plantations, 60; blacks calling for abolishing, 60–61
Cox Road, Christ Church parish, 31; size and date of formation for, 109*a*
Crab Hill, St Lucy parish, 53; size and date of formation for, 116*a*
Craig, Susan, 2
Crawford, Wynter, 99
Crawford Land, 65
Crick, St Lucy parish, size and date of formation for, 123*a*
Crown Land, 15
Curiosity Village, St James parish, 54
Curiosity, St James parish, size and date of formation for, 114*a*

Danesbury, St Michael parish, 63; size and date of formation for, 116*a*

Dark Hole. *See* St Sylvans, St Joseph parish

Dash Valley, St George parish, size and date of formation for, 110*a*

Date Tree Hill, St Peter parish, size and date of formation for, 124*a*

Davy, John, 15, 89, 93

Dayrell, Callop (Caleb), 37, 38, 90

Dayrells Road, Christ Church parish, 29, 56; size and date of formation for, 109*a*; villages formed along corridors, 64; village formed through private treaty arrangements, 46

Deacons Rd., St Michael parish, 63; size and date of formation for, 116*a*

Dean's Village, St James parish, size and date of formation for, 121*a*

Deighton's Rd., St Michael parish, size and date of formation for, 124*a*

Derricks, St James parish, size and date of formation for, 121*a*

Diamond, St Philip parish, size and date of formation for, 125*a*

Diamond Corner, St Peter parish: as a large village, 54; size and date of formation for, 117*a*

Diamond Valley, St Philip parish, size and date of formation for, 118*a*

distribution of free villages across the island, 87

Dodson Land, 65

Dorants, St Andrew parish, as a principal village, 54; size and date of formation for, 113*a*

Douglin, John Christopher, land bequest in will of, 31–32

Douglin, Philip Henry, 32

Douglin Village, St Andrew parish, 31–32; size and date of formation for, 109*a*

Downs, St Philip parish, size and date of formation for, 118*a*

Dowridge, Archibald, 60

Draxes/Drakes, St Philip parish, size and date of formation for, 118*a*

Duncans, St Philip parish, size and date of formation for, 111*a*

Dunn, Richard, 18

Durants, St James parish, 80; size and date of formation for, 121*a*

Durhams, St Lucy parish, 57; size and date of formation for, 116*a*

Eagle Hall, St Michael parish, 63; size and date of formation for, 116*a*

East Lynn plantation, St George parish, 82; size and date of formation for, 120*a*

Eastcott, St Michael parish, 58
Eckstein Village, St Michael parish, size and date of formation for, 116*a*
Edey, Richard, 38
Edey's Village, Christ Church parish, size and date of formation for, 119*a*
Edey's Village, St John parish, size and date of formation for, 115*a*
Edge Cliff, St John parish, 83; size and date of formation for, 122*a*
Eisner, Gisela, 2
Elcocks, St Lucy parish, size and date of formation for, 123*a*
election of 1848, 8; impact of Rock Hall, St Michael parish on, 40–41, 89
elections and free villages, 95–97
"elite slaves", and founding of free villages, 89–90
Ellcock, Reynold Alleyne, 37, 39
Ellcock Bequest, Rock Hall and Bridgefield founded with funds from, 39
Ellerton plantation, St George parish, 82; size and date of formation for, 120*a*
Ellis, John Thomas, 58
emancipated people: civil bondage of, 22; as founders of free villages, 86, 88–91; importance of plantation labour for, 29. *See also* freedmen and women

emancipation: free villages allowed for actualization of, 84, 91; free village development and, 14, 26
Emerton/Blades, St Philip parish, size and date of formation for, 118*a*
emigration, 20–22, 64, 94, 100
employment opportunities, 69, 94
Endeavour Village/Orange Hill, St James parish, land acquired through communal action, 37, 38; size and date of formation for, 110*a*
enslaved people: listed in civil registration records, 6–7; master relationship with, 47; ranking of, 89–90
Enterprise, Christ Church parish, 80
Enterprise plantation, Christ Church parish, 74
Evelyn, George, 72, 75
environmental factors contributing to free village development, 81, 87
environmental features of high-density free villages, 78–79
Evergreen Grove, Christ Church parish, size and date of formation for, 112*a*

Fairfield & Tudor Bridge, St Michael parish, size and date of formation for, 124*a*
family villages, 31, 32
family subdivision of land, 84–85

Farm, St Michael parish:
  developed via land
  speculator Chapman,
  44; early farming lots
  established, 26; uniquely
  large size of, 45
Farm plantation, St Peter
  parish, 82
Farm plantation, St Thomas
  parish, 39
Farm Rd., St Philip parish, size
  and date of formation for,
  118*a*
Farm Rd. & Tenantry, St Peter
  parish, size and date of
  formation for, 124*a*
Farmers Village, St Joseph
  parish, size and date of
  formation for, 115*a*
Farley, Rawle, 2
farming lots, 40, 44, 45,
  62–63; conversion into
  house-spots, 84–85; early
  establishment of, 26–27
farming system used on free
  village lots, 92–94
First Step, St George parish,
  size and date of formation
  for, 114*a*
Fitts Village, St James parish,
  size and date of formation
  for, 110*a*
Flat Rock/Mess House, St
  George parish, 53; size and
  date of formation for, 114*a*
Flint Hall Gap, St Michael
  parish, size and date of
  formation for, 116*a*
formation of free villages: dates
  of, 109*a* –125*a;* procedures
  for, 45–46

Forde's Land, 64
Foster Lodge, St George parish,
  size and date of formation
  for, 120*a*
Foul Bay, Christ Church parish:
  free villages in, 52; poor
  white settlement at, 17;
  sparse settlement of, 15
founders of free villages, 88–91
Four Cross Rds., St John parish,
  size and date of formation
  for, 122*a*
Four Roads, St Philip parish,
  size and date of formation
  for, 125*a*
franchise: family welfare over
  the, 64, 96; at Rock Hall
  increased opportunity to
  exercise the, 42; villagers
  qualifying for the, 95–96
Franklin, Ann, 9
Friendly Cot, Christ Church
  parish, size and date of
  formation for, 109*a*
Free Hill, St Andrew parish, size
  and date of formation for,
  113*a*
Free Hill, St George parish, size
  and date of formation for,
  114*a*
Free Hill, St Lucy parish, size
  and date of formation for,
  110*a*, 116*a*
Free Hill, St Michael parish, 63;
  size and date of formation
  for, 116*a*
Free Hill/St Bernard's Village, St
  Joseph parish, size and date
  of formation for, 110*a*
Free Trade Act, 55

freeholders, constraints on in 1842, 24
free village development, first phase of, 21, 26; around Anglican and Methodist churches, 30; bequest villages, 30–37; and communal action, 37–38; constraints on, 15–17; growth of during, 88; lack of land settlement schemes, 29–30; and land speculation, 38–46; land transfer agencies, 29–30; located on marginal lands, 27; location, number, type and size of first free villages, 28*t;* map of first free villages, 27*f;* no official support for, 62; number, size, and date of formation, 109*a*–112*a;* price of land as constraint on, 23; and private treaty arrangement, 46–47; and self-help activities, 37; size of holdings, 27–28; socio-economic factors influencing development of, 11. *See also* Chapman, Peter; freeholders, constraints on in 1842
free village development, second phase of (1870–1905): and average size of holdings, 52; bottom tier parishes during, 54; community response to, 55; distribution of villages according to number of holdings, 51*t;* through increased number of and intensified settlement within, 63–64; factors contributing to, 55–57, 62; intensification of free village development, 48, 62–63; map of increase of, 49*f;* number, size, and date of formation, 112*a*–125*a;* numbers and acreage of newly formed, 48*t;* through private treaty arrangements, 59–62; six parishes where increase occurred, 50; size of, 55; in St Michael parish, 63–64; subdivision of small holdings, 64; wages linked to, 56; Workmans, St George parish, 52, 63
free village development, third phase of (1905–45), 67–85; factors involved in land appropriation during, 69; holdings in third phase villages, 78*t;* land speculation during, 72; land redistribution during, 76; in low tier parishes of St Thomas, St John, St Andrew, and St Joseph, 82–84; map of free villages by 1945, 68*f;* in middle tier parishes of St George, St Peter, and St Philip, 81–82; number of villages, holdings and acreage (1905–45), 67*t;* planters holding on to plantations during, 60–70;

Index

remittances contributing to, 70–72; in top tier parishes of St Michael, St James, Christ Church and St Lucy, 78–81
free village studies, 1–2; Halcrow and Cave's working definition of a free village, 11
free villages, 2–3; author questions popular opinion in Barbados regarding existence of, 1; classification of based on number of holdings, 78; creation process of new, 64–65; definition of, 10–11; and demand for land by blacks, 60; distribution of across the island, 87; distribution of villages according to number of holdings, 51*t*; economic role played by, 91–95; founders of, 88–91; intensification of settlement, 62–63; land bequests by William Reece initiating earliest, 35–36; identification of, 14; impact of voters on 1848 election from, 40–41; periods/phases in development of, 11–12; political impact from, 95–99; process of relocating from plantation to, 84–85; social impact from, 99–101; source material on history of, 3–9; three phases of development for, 24–25; tally of, 86*t*; voter registration campaign in, 40
free villages, economic role played by: allowed for occupational differentiation, 91; and farming, 92–94; benefits flowed from increase in population, 95; and remittances, 94–95; and spending power, 94
free villages, political impact from, 95–99; liberal politicians supported, 99; riots and violence over elections, 97–99; voter qualifications, 95–97
free villages, social impact from, 99–101; contribution to creating a professional class, 101; contribution to social modernization, 101; increased self-worth of residents, 99–100; labour relations improved, 99–100
free villagers: agricultural labourers and, 65; employed on plantations, 69; labour power of, 14; and repossession of land for non-payment, 46; role played in economic and political life of Barbados, 86, 91–101; social standing of, 98; vilification of, 89
freedmen and women: and conditions required for becoming independent farmers, 69; and control of their labour power,

11; effected by lack of subdivided plantation land for sale, 70; land appropriated by, 76–77; price of land exorbitant for, 75; remittances providing cash for, 71; subdivision of plantations resulting in small holdings for, 84. *See also* emancipated people; remittances

French Village, St Peter parish, size and date of formation for, 117*a*

Fruitful Hill, St Joseph parish, size and date of formation for, 115*a*

Fustic, St Lucy parish, size and date of formation for, 123*a*

Gall Hill, Christ Church parish, size and date of formation for, 119*a*

Gall Hill, St John parish, as a principal village, 54; size and date of formation for, 115*a*

(The) Garden, St James parish, size and date of formation for, 110*a*

gardens, 15

Gay's Land, St Peter parish, size and date of formation for, 111*a*

Gibbons Boggs, Christ Church parish, 35; size and date of formation for, 109*a*

Gibbons plantation, Christ Church parish, William Reece bequest of, 4

Gibbs, Bentley, 20

Gibsons & Pinketts, St Philip parish, size and date of formation for, 118*a*

Gilkes, St Lucy parish, size and date of formation for, 123*a*

Gilkes Village, St James parish, size and date of formation for, 121*a*

Gilkes' Village, St Michael parish, size and date of formation for, 124*a*

Gill, John Francis, 57

Glebe Land, St John parish, size and date of formation for, 122*a*

Glenburnie, St John parish, size and date of formation for, 115*a*

Glendlebrough, St Lucy parish, size and date of formation for, 123*a*

Gmelch, George, 9

Gmelch, Sharon, 9

Good Intent (Cane Hill), St George parish: developed via land speculator Chapman, 44; early farming lots established, 26

Goodland, St Michael parish, large size of, 79; size and date of formation for, 124*a*

Goodland plantation, St Michael parish, 75

Government Hill, St Michael parish, 52, 56, 63; size and date of formation for, 117*a;* villages formed along corridors, 64

Governor Hay, 61

Grant, John, 41
Grape Hall, St Lucy parish, size and date of formation for, 123*a*
Graveyard, St Lucy parish, 53; size and date of formation for, 116*a*
Grazettes, St Michael parish, size and date of formation for, 124*a*
Green, William, 2
Green Gardens, Christ Church parish, size and date of formation for, 112*a*
Green Hill, St Michael parish, 56; size and date of formation for, 117*a*; villages formed along corridors, 64
Greenfield, Sidney, 9, 31
Greenidge, Charles Joseph (land speculator), 58, 106*n*9
Greenidges (Second Step), St Lucy parish, 32; formed through land bequests, 34; size and date of formation for, 110*a*
Greens plantation, St George parish, 82
Greens, St George parish, size and date of formation for, 120*a*
Greenwich, St James parish, as a large village, 54, 59; size and date of formation for, 114*a*
Greenwich, subdivision of plantation land, 61
Grigg Field, St Lucy parish, size and date of formation for, 116*a*

Griffith, John, 97
Guyana (British Guiana), 29, 30; emigration of Barbados labour force to, 21; price of land, 23; proprietary villages in, 30; remittances from, 56, 94

Haggatt Hall, St Michael parish: growth of during first phase, 88; large size of, 79; size and date of formation for, 111*a*, 124*a*
Halcrow, M. and J.M. Cave *(Peasant Agriculture in Barbados)*, 12; deficiencies in data of, 87; statistics on sugar cane output (1940–46), 92–93; working definition of a free village, 11
"half castes", 89
Half Moon Fort, St Lucy parish, size and date of formation for, 123*a*
Hall, Catherine, 1
Hall, Douglas, 2
Halls, St Lucy parish, size and date of formation for, 123*a*
Halls Rd., St Michael parish, size and date of formation for, 117*a*
Halls Village, St James parish, size and date of formation for, 114*a*
Harlington, St Philip parish, size and date of formation for, 118*a*
Harmony Cottage, St George parish, size and date of formation for, 120*a*

Harmony Hall, Christ Church parish, 34; size and date of formation for, 109*a*

Harrises, St Lucy parish, size and date of formation for, 123*a*

Hastings, Christ Church parish, size and date of formation for, 112*a*

Hastings, St Michael parish, 56; villages formed along corridors, 64

Hay (Governor), 61

Heddings, St Philip parish, size and date of formation for, 125*a*

Hermill, St James parish, 54

Hewitt, Samuel Francis, 99

Higginsons, St Lucy parish, size and date of formation for, 123*a*

Highlands, St Philip parish, size and date of formation for, 125*a*

Hillaby, St Thomas parish, size and date of formation for, 125*a*

Hillaby plantation, St Thomas parish, 83

Hillswick, St Joseph parish, size and date of formation for, 115*a*

Hinds Hill/Lodge Hill, St Michael parish, size and date of formation for, 117*a*

Holder, George Francis, 57

Holder's Hill, St James parish: registered voters in 1870s in, 96; size and date of formation for, 114*a*

Holder's Village, St George parish, size and date of formation for, 114*a*

holdings within villages: distribution of villages according to number of, 51*t*; factors accounting for large number of, 78–82; holdings in third phase villages, 78*t*; parishes grouped by number of, 78; size of, 85

Holetown, black Barbadians residing in, 84

Holt, Thomas, 2

Hope Road (& Bridge), St Lucy parish, 81; size and date of formation for, 123*a*

Hopewell, Christ Church parish, size and date of formation for, 119*a*

Horse Hill, St Joseph parish, size and date of formation for, 122*a*

Hothersal Turning, St Michael parish, 29, 56, 63; villages formed along corridors, 64

house-spots: family cohesion over economic interests when creating, 42, 84–85; farming lots evolving into, 63, 84–85; land division in Rock Hall creating, 41; new villages of 1900s little more than, 79

Howard's Hill, St John parish, size and date of formation for, 122*a*

Howell's Cross Roads, St Michael parish, 52; size and date of formation for, 117*a*

Index

Hoyte's Village, St Andrew parish, size and date of formation for, 113*a*
Humphrey's Hill, St John parish, size and date of formation for, 122*a*

immigration. *See* emigration; migration
indentured servants, 17, 23
Indian Ground, St Andrew parish, size and date of formation for, 120*a*
Indian Ground, St Peter parish, size and date of formation for, 117*a*
industrial conflict (1838–40), 22
Industry Hall, Christ Church parish, size and date of formation for, 119*a*
inheritance practices, *places* surviving through, 18
installment principle ("accommodating terms"), 45–46, 76
internal migration, as factor for free village sites, 29
(The) Ivy, St Michael parish, 58, size and date of formation for, 117*a*

Jack ma' nanny Gap/Wavell Ave., St Michael parish, size and date of formation for, 124*a*
Jackman, Robert, 38
Jackman's, St Michael parish, size and date of formation for, 124*a*
Jackson, St Thomas parish, size and date of formation for, 125*a*
Jackson's, St Michael parish, size and date of formation for, 124*a*
Jamaica, 29, 30, 73; free villages in, 10; "Negro Peasant Proprietors" in, 65; proprietary villages in, 30
Jericho/Near Jordans, St George parish, size and date of formation for, 114*a*
Jessamine Lane, St Philip parish, size and date of formation for, 118*a*
Jordans, St Lucy parish, size and date of formation for, 123*a*
Josey Hill, St Lucy parish, size and date of formation for, 110*a*

Kellman, John, 97
Kendal Hill, Christ Church parish, size and date of formation for, 119*a*
Kennedy, Patience, 32
Kew Land, St Thomas parish, size and date of formation for, 125*a*
kin networks, relocation from plantation to free villages through, 84
King, Dr William John, 45
Kirtons, St Philip parish, 72, 82; size and date of formation for, 125*a*
kitchen gardens, 15

Knibb, William, 13, 40; "free village" term used for Jamaican settlements by, 10, 103*n*18
Knight's Village, St John parish, size and date of formation for, 122*a*

labour, 19; contesting the terms of compensation for, 22; supply of for plantations, 29
labour power of free villagers, 14, 65; continued as plantation labourers, 85
labour supply, 22, 29, 61
labourers: and planter/employer relationship, 47; purchase of land by outsiders and effect on, 77; as typical purchaser of lots from Chapman, 45
land ownership, 13, 60; based on informal process, 31
land possession, 15
land prices, 23; lots compared to plantation land, 75
land settlement schemes, 61; lack of, 29–30
land shortage, 64
land speculation: as agency of land transfer, 58–60, 69, 71–76, 84, 88; controversy among elites regarding, 77–78; first phase of free village development and, 37, 38–47; in Christ Church, St Michael, St Lucy, St George and St James parishes, 76; not significant in St Joseph parish, 76

land speculators: drawn to St Michael parish, 79; during period of 1905-30s, 72–78; installment principle institutionalized by, 76; number and size of villages created by, 43*t*; subdivision of plantations leading to freedmen and women ownership, 84; unethical practices of, 74–76; unique definition of, 38. *See also* Chapman, Peter
land transfer: sold in plantation blocks, 62; and unethical practices of land speculators, 74–76. *See also* bequests of land and free villages
land transfer, agencies of, 29–30, 88; bequest villages as, 30–37; communal action acting as, 37–38; and land speculation, 38–47; self-help activities acting as, 37
landlords/landladies, new types of, 64–65
landowners, list of (1847), 4
"lands", definition of, 64
Lansdowne, Christ Church parish, size and date of formation for, 119*a*
large villages, 50
Lazaretto, St Michael parish, 79; size and date of formation for, 124*a*
Lead Vale, Christ Church parish, size and date of formation for, 109*a*
legislation; preservation of

Index

a plantation-dependent labour force through, 20–22
Lemon Grove, Christ Church parish, size and date of formation for, 112*a*
Less Beholden, St Lucy parish: registered voters in 1870s in, 96; size and date of formation for, 123*a*
Levy, Claude, 2
Liberal (Barbadian newspaper), 41; as source of information on free village development, 8
liberal politicians recruiting from free villages, 99
Licorish Gap, St Michael parish, 52; size and date of formation for, 117*a*
Licorish Village, St Andrew parish, size and date of formation for, 109*a*, 120*a*
line villages, 13, 104*n*1; suburban corridors in St Michael and Christ Church parishes, 56, 64
Little Hope, St Philip parish, 35
located labourer system, 21
Lodge Road, Christ Church parish, size and date of formation for, 109*a*
Lonesome Hill, St Peter parish, size and date of formation for, 117*a*
Lord, Elizabeth Sarsfield, 35
Lord, Samuel Hall, 35
Lonesome Hill, St Peter parish, 54
Lowenthal, David, 13
Lower Birneys, St Michael parish, size and date of formation for, 117*a*, 124*a*
Lower Carlton, St James parish, 80; size and date of formation for, 121*a*
Lowlands, St Lucy parish, size and date of formation for, 123*a*
Lyder Cottage, St Lucy parish, size and date of formation for, 123*a*
Lynch, James Challenor, land speculation professionalized by, 72, 73, 75, 82

Macaroni Town, St George parish, size and date of formation for, 114*a*
Mango Lodge, St Andrew parish, size and date of formation for, 120*a*
Manning, Sam, 58
Mannings Land, St George parish, size and date of formation for, 114*a*
Mapp, James Browne, 43*t;* land sales established Cherry Grove, St John parish, 43
Marchfield plantation, St Philip parish, 82; size and date of formation for, 125*a*
Market Hill, St George parish, 53, 58; size and date of formation for, 114*a*
Marley Vale, St Philip parish, size and date of formation for, 111*a*
Massiah St, St John parish, size and date of formation for, 110*a*

Maxwell Hill, Christ Church parish: size and date of formation for, 109*a;* village formed through private treaty arrangements, 46

Mayers, Samuel James, 43*t;* land sales established Cave Hill/Rock Dundo village, 43

Mayfield, St George parish, size and date of formation for, 120*a*

McClean's, St Lucy parish, size and date of formation for, 123*a*

McConney, Thomas Nathaniel (land speculator), 72, 73, 75

McLellan, George, 70

medium-sized villages, 50

Melrose/Shorey Village, St Thomas parish, size and date of formation for, 125*a*

Melverton, St George parish, size and date of formation for, 114*a*

Melvin's Hill, St Joseph parish, size and date of formation for, 115*a*

merchants, 55

Mess House Hill, St Thomas parish, size and date of formation for, 119*a*

method of analysis, 10–12

Methodism, land bequest to enslaved adults influence by, 35

Methodist churches, Barbadian villages around, 30

middle class, 77, 94

middle-class subdivision, The Ivy as a, 58

middle tier parishes, 50; definition of, 53

Middleton, St George parish, 59; size and date of formation for, 114*a*

migration 21; internally, 29; rural to urban, 56, 64; in St Joseph parish, 83; in St Philip parish, 82. *See also* emigration

Mile and Quarter, St Peter parish: as a large village, 54; size and date of formation for, 117*a*

militia tenants, 17, 23

Millington's, St Michael parish, 58

Millers Land, St John parish, size and date of formation for, 122*a*

Mimbo Jane (daughter of John Christopher Douglin), 32

mini-villages, 65

Mintz, Sidney, 1; variation on his "essential" conditions for status as independent farmers, 69

Moore, Brian, 2

Moore's Land, St John parish, size and date of formation for, 115*a*

mortgages, 46

(The) Mount, St Michael parish, size and date of formation for, 117*a*

Mount Clapham plantation, Christ Church parish, 9, 72, 75

Mount Standfast, St James parish, size and date of formation for, 121*a*

Mount Wilton plantation, 37, 39, 90
Mt. All, St Andrew parish, as a principal village, 54; size and date of formation for, 113*a*
Mt. Dacres, St Joseph parish, size and date of formation for, 122*a*
Mt. Friendship, St Michael parish, size and date of formation for, 117*a*
Mt. Hillaby, St Andrew parish, size and date of formation for, 113*a*
Mt. Johnson, St Lucy parish, size and date of formation for, 123*a*
Mt. Standfast, St James parish, 80
Mt. View, St Lucy parish, size and date of formation for, 123*a*
Munroe's Tenantry, St George parish, size and date of formation for, 114*a*
Murphy, Ralph Cyril, 58
Murrays place, St Philip parish, 43
My Lords Hill, St Michael parish, 29, 56, 63; size and date of formation for, 111*a*; villages formed along corridors, 64

"Negro Peasant Proprietors" *(Pall Mall Gazette)*, 65
naming of villages, significance of, 46–47, 52, 54

Near Apple Hall, St Philip parish, size and date of formation for, 117*a*
Near Bagatelle, St Thomas parish, size and date of formation for, 119*a*
Near Bayfield, St Philip parish, size and date of formation for, 117*a*
Near Belair, St Philip parish, size and date of formation for, 118*a*
Near Belfield, St Michael parish, size and date of formation for, 116*a*
Near Briggs, St Philip parish, size and date of formation for, 118*a*
Near Bushy Park, St Philip parish, size and date of formation for, 118*a*
Near Cane Garden, St Philip parish, size and date of formation for, 118*a*
Near Castle, St Peter parish, size and date of formation for, 124*a*
Near Clarke's Court, Christ Church parish, size and date of formation for, 112*a*
Near Collymore Rock, St Michael parish, size of small holdings in, 27
Near Crane, St Philip parish, size and date of formation for, 118*a*
Near Durants, Christ Church parish, size and date of formation for, 112*a*

Near Ealing Grove, Christ Church parish, size and date of formation for, 112*a*
Near Eastbourne, St Philip parish, size and date of formation for, 118*a*
Near East Point, St Philip parish, size and date of formation for, 118*a*
Near Ebenezer Church, St Philip parish, size and date of formation for, 118*a*
Near Enterprise, Christ Church parish: large number of holdings in, 51; size and date of formation for, 112*a*
Near Fair View, Christ Church parish, size and date of formation for, 112*a*
Near Fortescue, St Philip parish, size and date of formation for, 118*a*
Near Golden Grove, St Philip parish, size and date of formation for, 118*a*
Near Goodland, Christ Church parish, size and date of formation for, 112*a*
Near Grand View, St Philip parish, size and date of formation for, 118*a*
Near Greenland, Christ Church parish, size and date of formation for, 112*a*
Near Grove, St Philip parish, size and date of formation for, 118*a*
Near Hampden, St Philip parish, size and date of formation for, 125*a*
Near Hill House, Christ Church parish, size and date of formation for, 112*a*
Near Home, St Philip parish, size and date of formation for, 118*a*
Near Hope, St James parish, size and date of formation for, 114*a*
Near Hopeland, St Philip parish, size and date of formation for, 118*a*
Near Husbands, St Michael parish, size and date of formation for, 117*a*
Near Industry Hall, St Philip parish, size and date of formation for, 118*a*
Near Jones, St Philip parish, size and date of formation for, 118*a*
Near Kingsland, Christ Church parish, size and date of formation for, 112*a*
Near Kirtons, St Philip parish, size and date of formation for, 118*a*
Near Lears. *See* Bibby's Lane, St Michael parish
Near Loamfield, St Philip parish, size and date of formation for, 118*a*
Near Lodge, St Michael parish, size and date of formation for, 117*a*
Near Lowthers, Christ Church parish, size and date of formation for, 112*a*
Near Lyrias, Christ Church parish, size and date of formation for, 112*a*

Index 157

Near Mangrove, St Philip parish, size and date of formation for, 118*a*

Near Maynards, Christ Church parish, size and date of formation for, 112*a*

Near Montrose, Christ Church parish, size and date of formation for, 112*a*

Near Mt. Clapham, Christ Church parish, size and date of formation for, 112*a*

Near Newton, Christ Church parish, size and date of formation for, 112*a*

Near Oldbury, St Philip parish, size and date of formation for, 118*a*

Near Oughterson, St Philip parish, size and date of formation for, 118*a*

Near Oxnards, St James parish, size and date of formation for, 115*a*

Near Packers, Christ Church parish, size and date of formation for, 112*a*

Near Pegwell, Christ Church parish, size and date of formation for, 112*a*

Near Plum Grove, Christ Church parish, size and date of formation for, 112*a*

Near Pounders, St Philip parish, size and date of formation for, 118*a*

Near Prospect, St James parish, size and date of formation for, 115*a*

Near Rices, St Philip parish, size and date of formation for, 118*a*

Near Ruby, St Philip parish, size and date of formation for, 118*a*

Near Sandford, St Philip parish, size and date of formation for, 119*a*

Near Searles, Christ Church parish, size and date of formation for, 113*a*

Near Social Hall, Christ Church parish, size and date of formation for, 113*a*

Near Spencers, St Philip parish, size and date of formation for, 119*a*

Near Spring Garden, St Michael parish, size and date of formation for, 117*a*

Near St. David's, Christ Church parish, size and date of formation for, 113*a*

Near St Helens, St George parish, size and date of formation for, 114*a*

Near St Martin's Church, St Philip parish, size and date of formation for, 119*a*

Near The Risk, St Peter parish, size and date of formation for, 117*a*

Near Thicket, St Philip parish, size and date of formation for, 119*a*

Near Union Hall, St Philip parish, size and date of formation for, 119*a*

Near Vineyard, St Philip parish, size and date of formation for, 119*a*
Near Walkers, St George parish, 53
Near Wanstead, St Michael parish, size and date of formation for, 117*a*
Near Warners, Christ Church parish, large number of holdings in, 51–52; size and date of formation for, 113*a*
Near Welches, Christ Church parish, size and date of formation for, 113*a*
Near Welches, St Michael parish, size and date of formation for, 117*a*
Near Well House, St Philip parish, size and date of formation for, 119*a*
Near Woodbourne, Christ Church parish, size and date of formation for, 113*a*
Near Wotton, Christ Church parish, size and date of formation for, 113*a*
Near Yorkshire, Christ Church parish, size and date of formation for, 113*a*
Nesfield, St Lucy parish, 53; size and date of formation for, 116*a*
"new freedmen", 69. *See also* freedmen and women
"new villages", 103*n*18
Newbury, St George parish, 53, 59; large number of holdings in, 52; size and date of formation for, 114*a*; subdivision of plantation land, 61
newspapers, as source of information on free village development, 8
Newstead, St Peter parish, size and date of formation for, 124*a*
Nicholls' Village, St James parish, size and date of formation for, 121*a*
nigger yard, 15, 54
Nonconformist churches, 99
non-plantation tenantries, 64
Northumberland, St Lucy parish, size and date of formation for, 110*a*
Nowell Village, St Joseph parish, size and date of formation for, 115*a*
Nurse, William John, 33
(The) Nursery, St Philip parish, 31, 33; holdings at (1875), 33*t;* size and date of formation for, 111*a*

occupational differentiation, 91
official records, as source of information on free village formation, 3–
officials, free villages unacknowledged by, 49
Oistins, black Barbadians residing in, 84
Old Post Office, St George parish, 53; size and date of formation for, 114*a*
O'Neal, Charles Duncan, 99
O'Neal's, St Michael parish, 58
oral tradition, history of free villages based on, 14

Orange Grove, St Joseph parish, size and date of formation for, 115*a*

Outram, Robert Thomas, 43*t*; land sales established Waverley Cot, St George parish and Murrays place, St Philip parish, 43

Overton, St Joseph parish, size and date of formation for, 122*a*

owner-occupier, questions of, 14

Padmore Village, St Thomas parish, size and date of formation for, 125*a*

Paget, Hugh, 2

Pall Mall Gazette, 65

Panama, remittances from, 70, 94

Panama Canal, Barbadians migrating to work on, 11

Panama Money, inflow of, 48, 70–72, 95

Paradise Village, Christ Church parish, 34; size and date of formation for, 120*a*

Paradise Village, St George parish, size and date of formation for, 121*a*

Parish Land, Christ Church parish, size and date of formation for, 120*a*

Parish Land, St George parish, size and date of formation for, 121*a*

parish rate books, 12; for St Michael parish, 26, 27

parishes, ranking of according to size and number of free villages, 50, 78–79

Parris Hill, St Joseph parish, size and date of formation for, 110*a*

peasant agriculture, surveys of, 5–6

Peasant Agriculture in Barbados (Halcrow and Cave, 1944/1947), 6

peasant proprietary: endorsement for limited number of, 71; government preventing rise of a, 60; news article on, 65; in St James parish, 79–80

peasantry, 1; public endorsement of, 71

peasants loan bank, 76

Penny Hole, sparse settlement of, 15

Petersys, St Lucy parish, size and date of formation for, 123*a*

Phillips, T.O., 76–77

physiographic areas of Barbados, map of, 16*f*

Pile, A.J. (plantocrat), 59, 61

Pilgrim, Eustace Graham, 72, 74, 75; land speculation activity by, 79–80

Pilgrim Road/Pilgrim Place, Christ Church parish, 35

Pilgrim Place, Christ Church parish, 74, 80; size and date of formation for, 109*a*; William Reece bequest at plantation of, 4

Piper's Hill, St Michael parish, size and date of formation for, 124*a*

places (land units), as sites of new villages, 17–18
plantation labour, traditional workforce of, 19
plantation land, 13, 17; "elite slaves" gaining portions of, 90; free villages located outside of, 14; labour supply for, 29; proximity of free villages to, 51, 55; release of marginal land from, 59–60; sold intact, 70, 77; subdivision of, 61–62, 71, 77; villagers labouring on, 65, 69. *See also* sugar plantations
plantation society: threats to, 55; and loss of patronage in post-slavery era, 57; existing alongside a peasant proprietary, 71
plantation tenantries, 13–14, 21, 54, 65; Colonial Office required to provide information on, 4–5; escape of through creation of house-spots, 42; majority moved to free villages in third stage of development, 69; relocation to free villages from, 84. *See also* located labourer system
plantations: crisis during 1880s to WWI, 69–70; land speculators buying indebted, 74; labour supply unaffected by increase in free villages, 85; large villages replacing, 59
planters, 11, 13, 15, 19, 59–60; against small farms, 18; British government undermining interests of, 20; creating a dependent labour force, 21; debt resulting from depression in sugar industry, 69–70; facilitating inadvertently free village development, 47; land bequests to enslaved paramours and children, 17; opposition to small land holdings, 22–23; primogeniture ignored by, 57; unconscious promotion of village formation, 56–57. *See also* small planters
planter's parish, definition of a, 83
policymakers, blacks' proposals on land transfers blocked by, 61
population increase on free villages, 95
poor-white settlements, 17, 23
Porters, St James parish, 80; size and date of formation for, 121*a*
Potato Riot at Boscobel plantation (1895), 89, 98
praedial larceny, 77
pre-emancipation villages, 19*t*
Prerogative, St George parish, size and date of formation for, 121*a*
Prerogative plantation, St George parish, 82
Prescod, Samuel Jackman, 22, 46, 99; founded the Liberal Party, 8, 40, 41; owner of the *Liberal*, 8
Price, Quaco, 34

Price, Sarah, 34
Price, William Malloney, 34
price gouging, 46
primogeniture, 57
principal villages, 52–53; identified by the Water Supply Commission (1885), 5; in St George parish, 53
private treaty arrangements, villages formed through, 37, 46–47, 59–63, 88
profits from plantation land sales, 77
Progressive League (Barbados Labour Party), 99
proprietary villages: in Christ Church parish, 35; lack of in Barbados, 30
Prospect, St James parish, as a large village, 54
Prospect, St Michael parish, 58
protests by free villagers (1880s–90s), 98–99
provision crops, 92

quantitative data, importance of as a source of information on free village development, 12
Queen St., St Peter parish, size and date of formation for, 124*a*

rab land, 17
Ramparts, St Michael parish, 63; identified as a principal village, 52; size and date of formation for, 117*a*
rate books. *See* parish rate books

Rawlins/Rollins, Christ Church parish, size and date of formation for, 113*a*
records, lost for six parishes, 65
"Redleg" village, Foul Bay, Christ Church parish as a, 52
Redmans Village, St Thomas parish: established as a village, 38; land acquired through communal action, 37; registered voters in 1870s in, 96; size and date of formation for, 111*a*
red-soil district, 54
Reece, William, 35; apparent ignorance of bequest by, 4
Retreat, St Lucy parish, size and date of formation for, 123*a*
Retreat, St Peter parish, size and date of formation for, 117*a*
Retreat/Near Hilbury, St George parish, size and date of formation for, 114*a*
Retreat Wood, St George parish, size and date of formation for, 114*a*
Reeves, Conrad (Chief Justice), 61
Reeves Hill, St James parish, size and date of formation for, 121*a*
Reids Bay/ Weston, St James parish, 80; size and date of formation for, 121*a*
remittances, 9, 11, 25, 56, 69; economic role played by in free villages, 94–95; from "Panama Money", 70–72;

from the United States, 70; role of land speculators and, 74–75, 80
resident status in free villages, 65
Richardson, Bonham, 95
Ridgeway plantation, St Thomas, 39
riots, 97–98
(The) Risk, St Lucy parish, 35; size and date of formation for, 123*a*
River Bay, St Lucy parish, size and date of formation for, 116*a*
Roaches, St George parish, size and date of formation for, 114*a*
Roaches, St Lucy parish, size and date of formation for, 116*a*
Road View, St Peter parish, size and date of formation for, 124*a*
Roberts, George, 21, 70, 71
Roberts, St Michael parish, early farming lots established, 26
Roberts Tenantry (Near Neils), St Michael parish, 44; size and date of formation for, 111*a*
(The) Rock/ Spooners Hill, St Michael parish, size and date of formation for, 117*a*
Rock Dundo, St James parish, size and date of formation for, 121*a*
Rock Dundo, St Michael parish, size and date of formation for, 111*a*
Rock Hall, St Andrew parish, 83; size and date of formation for, 120*a*
Rock Hall, St George parish, 53
Rock Hall, St Lucy parish, 53; size and date of formation for, 116*a*
Rock Hall, St Philip parish, size and date of formation for, 111*a*
Rock Hall, St Thomas, 72; conversion of farming lots to house-spots, 84–85; an early free village, 1; early farming lots at, 26; founders of, 90; the franchise exercised at, 64; house-spots provided for kin from plantation tenantry, 41–42; impact on 1848 election of voters from, 41, 89; registered voters in 1870s in, 96; significance of formation of village at, 40; size and date of formation for, 111*a;* sociological significance of, 41–42; uniquely large size of, 45; village formed through a one-off land speculation, 39; voting qualifications unmet by residents of, 96
Rock Hall/Near St Helens, St George parish, size and date of formation for, 114*a*
Rock Hall/Near Walkers, St George parish, size and date of formation for, 114*a*
Rock Hall plantation, failure of due to poor soil, 40

Rockfield, St Lucy parish, size and date of formation for, 123*a*

Rockley, Christ Church parish, 80; size and date of formation for, 120*a*

Rodney, Walter, 2

Roebuck St., St John parish, size and date of formation for, 122*a*

Rose Hill, St Peter parish, size and date of formation for, 124*a*

Rose Hill/Silver Hill, Christ Church parish: size and date of formation for, 109*a*; village formed through private treaty arrangements, 46

Roses, St Philip parish, size and date of formation for, 125*a*

Rouen, St Michael parish, 52, 58; size and date of formation for, 117*a*

Round Rock, Christ Church parish, size and date of formation for, 113*a*

Rucks, Christ Church parish, size and date of formation for, 113*a*

Rugby plantation, 37

rural life studies, lack of detailed analysis in, 2

rural population, free village development and changes in, 67

rural to urban migration, 64

Rycrofts, Christ Church parish, size and date of formation for, 120*a*

Saint, Dr John, 76–77

Salmonds, St Lucy parish, size and date of formation for, 123*a*

Salters, St George parish, size and date of formation for, 121*a*

Salters plantation, St George parish, 81

Sandy Hill, St Philip parish, size and date of formation for, 119*a*

Sargeants Village, poor white settlement at, 17

Sarjeant St., St John parish, size and date of formation for, 110*a*

Sarjeants Village, Christ Church parish, 34

Sayes Court, Christ Church parish, size and date of formation for, 120*a*

Scarborough, Christ Church parish, size and date of formation for, 120*a*

scholarly work: lack of detailed accounts on post-slavery in Barbados in, 2; as source of information on free village development, 9

Sea View, Christ Church parish, size and date of formation for, 120*a*

Sea View, St James parish, 80; size and date of formation for, 121*a*

Sea View, St Philip parish, size and date of formation for, 119*a*

Sealy, James, 33

Sealy Hall, St John parish, size and date of formation for, 122*a*

Sebastien, Raphael, 2

settlement patterns of free villages, 11, 17; altered during third phase of development, 84

Sewell, W.G., 22, 89, 91, 94

Scotland District, St Andrew and St Joseph parishes, sparse settlement of, 15, 83

Schomburgk, Robert, 17

Sherbourne, St John parish, 83; size and date of formation for, 122*a*

Shermans, St Lucy parish, size and date of formation for, 123*a*

Shermans, St Peter parish, size and date of formation for, 124*a*

Shop Hill, St Thomas parish, 54

shopkeepers and free villages, 91

Shorey Village, St Andrew parish, size and date of formation for, 110*a*, 120*a*

Shufflers Village, St Joseph parish, size and date of formation for, 115*a*

Silver Sands, Christ Church parish, size and date of formation for, 120*a*

Sion Hill, St James parish, 80; size and date of formation for, 121*a*

Sisnett, G.W., 49

Six Roads, St Philip parish, size and date of formation for, 119*a*

size of holdings, 85

size of village sites, 45

Skeete, C.C., 5, 75, 76, 89, 98

Skeetes Hill, Christ Church parish, size and date of formation for, 113*a*

small farm sector: in St Philip parish, 82; size of holding preventing emergence of, 69, 84–85

small-hold land ownership, 18; blocked through legislation, 21; planters against, 56; remittances contributing to, 71–72

smallholders: land bought with installment principle, 76; limited employment opportunities for, 69; majority not considered small farmers due to land constrictions, 85; and repossession of land for non-payment, 46; voting by, 41, 96

smallholdings, 1; early reports on development of, 4; early years, 26–27; price of land, 60, 75; settled policy against, 62; subdivision of, 64

small planters, contribution to free village development by, 56

Small Town, St John parish, size and date of formation for, 122*a*

small villages, 50

Smith, M.G., 31

Smith, Raymond, 1

social gradients, creation of, 65
Social Hall plantation, 37, 90
source material on free villages in Barbados recovered through: civil registration records, 6–7; landowner lists, 4; newspapers, 8; official records, 3–4; oral tradition, 14; "principal" villages of 1885, 5; scholarly work, 9; surveyors' plats, 9; surveys of peasant agriculture, 5–6; taxpayer and voter records, 7, 14; wills and deeds, 7–8, 12, 14
South District, St George parish, size and date of formation for, 114*a*
South View, Christ Church parish, size and date of formation for, 113*a*
Southerland Hill, St Lucy parish, size and date of formation for, 116*a*
Speighstown, black Barbadians residing in, 84
Spooner's, St John parish, as a principal village, 54; size and date of formation for, 115*a*
Spout Farm, St Lucy parish, size and date of formation for, 116*a*
Spring Farm, St Thomas parish, size and date of formation for, 125*a*
Spring Garden, St Michael parish, 63
Springer, Horatio Nelson, 97
St Andrew parish: as bottom tier, 54; distribution of villages according to number of holdings within villages, 51*t*; first free villages listed by number, type and size in, 28*t*; growth of free villages during first phase in, 88; holdings in third phase villages in, 78*t*; list of landowners (1847) lacking for, 4; number and size of bequest villages in, 36*t*; number, size, and date of formation of villages in, 109*a*, 113*a*, 120*a*; number of villages, holdings and acreage (1905–45), 67*t*; pre-emancipation villages in, 19*t*; size of holdings in, 85; tally of free villages in, 86*t*; village development during third phase, 83; villages formed through land bequests, 34
St Barnabas, St Michael parish, 29; villages formed along corridors, 64
St Barnanas: church, 30, as village, 29, 56
St Christopher, Christ Church parish, size and date of formation for, 120*a*
St George parish, 64; characterized as a planter's parish, 83; distribution of villages according to number of holdings within villages, 51*t*; early farming lots established in, 26; first free villages listed by

number, type and size in, 28*t;* as a first tier parish, 53; free villages in, 49, 51; growth of free villages during first phase in, 88; high concentration of free villages in, 87; holdings in third phase villages in, 78*t;* land speculation resulting in free villages in, 43–44; large villages situated in, 52; as middle tier, 81; number, size, and date of formation of villages in, 110*a*, 113*a*–114*a*, 120*a*–121*a;* number of villages, holdings and acreage (1905–45), 67*t;* planters holding on to plantations in, 60–70; pre-emancipation villages in, 19*t;* sparse free village settlement in, 28; subdivision of Salters plantation, 81; tally of free villages in, 86*t*

St George Valley, sparse free village settlement on, 28

St George Vestry chairman, 5

St James parish: as bottom tier, 54; distribution of villages according to number of holdings within villages, 51*t;* climb to top tier regarding holdings and villages, 79; environmental features of high-density free villages in, 78–79; first free villages listed by number, type and size in, 28*t;* holdings in third phase villages in, 78*t*, 80–81*;* number, size, and date of formation of villages in, 110*a*, 114*a*–115*a*, 121*a;* number of villages, holdings and acreage (1905–45), 67*t;* pre-emancipation villages in, 19*t;* settlement patterns altered during third phase of development seen in, 84; size of holdings larger than other parishes, 85; tally of free villages in, 86*t*

St John parish, 7; as bottom tier, 54; characterized as a planter's parish, 83; distribution of villages according to number of holdings within villages, 51*t;* first free villages listed by number, type and size in, 28*t;* growth of free villages minimal during first phase in, 88; holdings in third phase villages in, 78*t;* number and size of bequest villages in, 36*t;* number, size, and date of formation of villages in, 110*a*, 115*a*, 121*a*–122*a;* number of villages, holdings and acreage (1905–45), 67*t;* planters holding on to plantations in, 60–70; pre-emancipation villages in, 19*t;* sparse free village settlement in, 28; tally of free villages in, 86*t;* villages established during third phase in, 82–83

St Joseph parish: distribution of villages according to number of holdings within villages, 51*t;* first free villages listed by number, type and size in, 28*t;* growth of free villages minimal during first phase in, 88; holdings in third phase villages in, 78*t;* as a middle tier parish, 53; number and size of bequest villages in, 36*t;* number, size, and date of formation of villages in, 110*a*, 115*a*, 122*a;* number of villages, holdings and acreage (1905–45), 67*t;* outmigration in, 83; pre-emancipation villages in, 19*t;* tally of free villages in, 86*t;* village development during third phase, 83

St Jude's, St George parish, size and date of formation for, 110*a*

St Lawrence, Christ Church parish, 34

St Lucy parish: distribution of villages according to number of holdings within villages, 51*t;* election upset in 1865, 97; environmental features of high-density free villages in, 78–79; first free villages listed by number, type and size in, 28*t;* high concentration of free villages in, 87; holdings in third phase villages in, 78*t,* 80; as a middle tier parish, 53; number and size of bequest villages in, 36*t;* number, size, and date of formation of villages in, 110*a*, 116*a*, 122*a*–123*a;* number of villages, holdings and acreage (1905–45), 67*t;* pre-emancipation villages in, 19*t;* tally of free villages in, 86*t*

St Matthias, Christ Church parish, size and date of formation for, 120*a*

St Michael parish, 7; distribution of villages according to number of holdings within villages, 51*t;* early farming lots established in, 26; environmental features of high-density free villages in, 78–79; expansion of free villages in, 50–52, 63–64; first free villages listed by number, type and size in, 28*t;* as a first tier parish, 52; free villages on marginal lands of, 28; growth of during, 88; growth of free villages during first phase in, 88; high concentration of free villages in, 87; holdings in third phase villages in, 78*t,* 80–81; land speculation resulting in free villages in, 43–44; number and size of bequest villages in, 36*t;* number, size, and date of formation of villages in, 111*a*, 116*a*–117*a,* 124*a;*

number of villages, holdings and acreage (1905–45), 67*t;* pre-emancipation villages in, 19*t;* rural to urban migration in, 64; settlement patterns altered during third phase of development seen in, 84; number of holdings larger than other parishes, 85; subdivision of plantations in, 73; suburban expansion in, 56; tally of free villages in, 86*t;* voter registration in, 40

St Patrick's, Christ Church parish: size and date of formation for, 109*a;* village formed through private treaty arrangements, 46

St Peter parish: as bottom tier, 54; distribution of villages according to number of holdings within villages, 51*t;* first free villages listed by number, type and size in, 28*t;* holdings in third phase villages in, 78*t;* as middle tier, 81; number and size of bequest villages in, 36*t;* number, size, and date of formation of villages in, 111*a*, 117*a*, 124*a;* number of villages, holdings and acreage (1905–45), 67*t;* subdivision of plantations in, 81; tally of free villages in, 86*t*

St Philip parish, 26, 27; bequests of land through in-family transfer, 31; distribution of villages according to number of holdings within villages, 51*t;* expansion of free villages in, 50–52; first free villages listed by number, type and size in, 28*t;* as a first tier parish, 52; growth of villages slower in, 82; holdings in third phase villages in, 78*t;* as middle tier, 81–82; number and size of bequest villages in, 36*t;* number, size, and date of formation of villages in, 111*a*, 117*a*–119*a*, 125*a;* number of villages, holdings and acreage (1905–45), 67*t;* pre-emancipation villages in, 19*t;* size of holdings in, 85; small farming sector in, 82; tally of free villages in, 86*t*

St Simon's, St Andrew parish, 83; growth of during first phase, 88; size and date of formation for, 110*a*, 120*a*

St Sylvans (Dark Hole), St Joseph parish, 53; registered voters in 1870s in, 96; size and date of formation for, 115*a*

St Thomas parish, 26; as bottom tier, 54; census information from 1851 limited for, 7; characterized as a planter's parish, 83; distribution of villages according to number of holdings within villages, 51*t;* election upset of 1848–49, 97; first free villages listed by number, type and size in, 28*t;*

holdings in third phase villages in, 78*t;* number and size of bequest villages in, 36*t;* number, size, and date of formation of villages in, 111*a*, 119*a*, 125*a;* number of villages, holdings and acreage (1905–45), 67*t;* planters holding on to plantations in, 60–70; pre-emancipation villages in, 19*t;* size of holdings in, 85; sparse free village settlement in, 28; tally of free villages in, 86*t;* voter registration in, 40
Starkey, O.P., 75, 77, 79
Station Hill, St Michael parish, 29, 56; villages formed along corridors, 64
Straughan, Thomas Henry, 57
Straughan's Village, St Joseph parish, 57; size and date of formation for, 115*a*
Streate, James William, 35
Stewarts Hill, St John parish, size and date of formation for, 115*a*
Stone Hall, St Philip parish, size and date of formation for, 119*a*
Stroude's Land, St Philip parish, size and date of formation for, 125*a*
subdivision, as activity of land speculators, 81. *See also* specific parishes
sugar cane: economic stability of, 55; grown on free village lots, 92–94

sugar cane industry, 47, 55, 59; depression in the, 69; importance for the colony, 19
"sugar cane sense", 93–94
Sugar Commission (1930), 77
Sugar Duties Act, 55
Sugar Hill, St Joseph parish, size and date of formation for, 115*a*
sugar plantations, 1; labour supply for, 29. *See also* plantation lands
Sugar Revolution, 16, 17; small properties surviving the, 18, 81
Sullivan, James, 42, 43*t*
Sunbury, St Peter parish, size and date of formation for, 124*a*
Superlative, St George parish, size and date of formation for, 121*a*
Superlative plantation, St George parish, 82
Supers Village (Suphir Hill), St Philip parish, 32; size and date of formation for, 111*a*
surveyors' plats, as source of information on free village development, 9
Sutton, Constance, 9
Swampy Town, St Lucy parish, 53; size and date of formation for, 116*a*
Sweet Bottom/Sweet Vale, poor white settlement at, 17
Sweet Field plantation, St Peter parish, 82
Sweet Home plantation, St Peter parish, 82

Taitt, Etheline, 9
Taitt's Hill, St George parish, size and date of formation for, 114*a*
taxpayers records, as source of information on free village development, 7
ten-acre men, 18
tenancy-at-will, 22
tenantry. *See* plantation tenantries
The Risk, St Philip parish, 35; size and date of formation for, 123*a*
third phase villages. *See* free village development, third phase of (1905–45)
Thornbury Hill, Christ Church parish, large number of holdings in, 51; size and date of formation for, 113*a*
Thorpes, St James parish, size and date of formation for, 121*a*
Thorpe's Cottage, St George parish, size and date of formation for, 121*a*
Times (newspaper), on election upset of 1865, 96, 97
Top Rock, Christ Church parish, size and date of formation for, 120*a*
top tier parishes, definition of, 50
Trinidad: emigration of Barbados labour force to, 21; price of land, 23; proprietary villages in, 30; remittances from, 56, 94

Triopath, St Andrew parish: poor white settlement at, 17; size and date of formation for, 113*a*
Trouillot, Michel-Rolph, 1
Turner's Hall Wood, 15
Turpin, Joseph, 90
Turpin, William, 37, 38, 90
Two Mile Hill, St Michael parish, size and date of formation for, 111*a;* size of small holdings in, 27

Under Mount Hill, St George parish, size and date of formation for, 114*a*
Union, St Joseph parish, size and date of formation for, 122*a*
United States, remittances from, 70
University of the West Indies, Barbados campus, research by undergraduates at, 9
Upper Carlton, St James parish, 80; size and date of formation for, 121*a*
Utility Village, St Michael parish, size and date of formation for, 117*a*

Valley, St Philip parish, size and date of formation for, 111*a*
Vaughans, St Joseph parish, 72
Vaughans Land, St Joseph parish, size and date of formation for, 122*a*
Vauxhall Village, Christ Church parish, 42; size and date of formation for, 109*a*

Venture, St John parish, 83; size and date of formation for, 122*a*
village shops, 99
villagers. *See* free villagers
village development, 14, 17; blocked through legislation, 21; constraints on, 24; *places* as site of, 18. *See also* free village development, first phase of; free village development, second phase of; free village development, third phase of
villages founded during pre-emancipation era, 19*t*
voter registration campaign, 41, 96
voting by villagers, 95. *See also* franchise
voting records, as source of information on free village development, 7

wage labour under plantation tenancy, 21; compared to high cost of land, 23
wages: decrease in prompting rural to urban migration, 56; of plantation labourer in the 1900s, 75
Wakenham, St Lucy parish, size and date of formation for, 123*a*
Walkers plantation, 44
Walker's Valley, St George parish, size and date of formation for, 121*a*

Walls, Christ Church parish, size and date of formation for, 113*a*
Walronds, Christ Church parish, size and date of formation for, 109*a*
waste lands, 15
Water Supply Commission, 1885 report on principle villages, 5
Water Street, Christ Church parish, size and date of formation for, 120*a*
Waterman's, St James parish, size and date of formation for, 121*a*
Watson, Athelstan (land speculator), 72–73, 75, 76; based out of Christ Church parish, 80; recognized importance of remittances, 74
Watts Tenantry, St George parish, size and date of formation for, 114*a*
Wavell Avenue, St Michael parish, 63
Waverly, Christ Church parish, size and date of formation for, 120*a*
Waverly Cot, St George parish, 43; size and date of formation for, 110*a*
Welch Town, St John parish, size and date of formation for, 122*a*
Welchman Hall, St Thomas parish, size and date of formation for, 125*a*

Welchman Hall plantation, St Thomas parish, 83
Welcome Hall, Christ Church parish, size and date of formation for, 113*a*
Wellfield, St Lucy parish, size and date of formation for, 123*a*
Westbury Rd, St Michael parish, size and date of formation for, 117*a*
West India Royal Commission (1897): complaints from blacks' representative to, 60–62; statistics on crisis within plantation lands, 70; support for subdivision of "sugar land", 62
West Indian National Congress Party, 99
Westbury Road, 52
Westmoreland, St James parish, 80; size and date of formation for, 121*a*
Weston, St James parish, size and date of formation for, 121*a*
Whapping, St James parish, size and date of formation for, 121*a*
(The) Whim, St Peter parish, size and date of formation for, 124*a*
(The) Whim plantation, St Peter parish, 82
White Hill, St Andrew parish, size and date of formation for, 113*a*
white villagers, low social status of, 23. *See also* poor-white settlements
Whitehall, St Michael parish, size and date of formation for, 111*a*, 124*a*
Whitehall, St Thomas parish, size and date of formation for, 111*a*
Whitehall plantation, 75
Wilcox, Christ Church parish, 74, 80; size and date of formation for, 120*a*
Wilkinson, J.L., 46
wills, 12, 103*n*13; and deeds, 7–8, 10, 12, 14, 50; history of free villages based on, 14; from Rock Hall, St Thomas parish, 42; providing for equal division among family members, 57; as source of information on free village development, 7–8, 26
Wilson Hill, St John parish, as a principal village, 54; size and date of formation for, 115*a*
Windsor Lodge, St Michael parish, 58
Windward Islands, price of land, 23
Windy Hill, St Thomas parish, 57
women as peasant proprietors, 80
Woodbourne, St Philip parish, size and date of formation for, 125*a*
woods, limited existence of, 15
Woodstock Village, St Michael parish, size and date of formation for, 117*a*

Work Hall, St Philip parish, 58; size and date of formation for, 119*a*

working class, 55–56

working-class village, The Ivy as a, 58

Workmans (Land), St George parish, 52; conversion of farming lots to house-spots, 84–85; developed via land speculator Chapman, 44; early farming lots established, 26; growth of during first phase, 88; registered voters in 1870s in, 96; size and date of formation for, 110*a;* uniquely large size of, 52, 45; voting qualifications unmet by residents of, 96

Worthing View, Christ Church parish, size and date of formation for, 120*a*

Wrong, Hume, 97

York Town, St James parish, size and date of formation for, 115*a*

Young, Allan, 2

Zores/Zoar, St John parish, 54; size and date of formation for, 115*a*

www.ingramcontent.com/pod-product-compliance
Lightning Source LLC
Chambersburg PA
CBHW022010160426
43197CB00007B/365